Mary Lou Kenworthy

Basenjis

Everything About History, Purchase, Care, Training, and Health

Filled with Full-color Photographs
Illustrations by Michele Earle-Bridges

BARRON'S

HISTORY AND ORIGIN OF THE BASENJI

The best way to have an enjoyable relationship with your Basenji is to understand his nature. This is a breed that has existed for thousands of years. Recent DNA studies classify the Basenji as one of the most primitive breeds. Insight into their personalities and idiosyncrasies can be gained by learning how they developed over time, where they came from and when, and what purpose they served in their native land.

Where Did the Basenji Come From?

The Basenji is an ancient natural breed that evolved in Africa, the cradle of the world for many species, including humans. Shaped by nature over thousands of years and culled by an environment where only the most adept survived, the Basenji comes to us in a form designed by its function. It was not until the nineteenth century, when Basenjis were brought out of Africa, that their breeding was artificially selected by man.

Their earliest recorded history is found in cave drawings, Egyptian tombs, and hieroglyphics. They were the palace dogs of the Pharaohs

A Basenji in a typical pose surveying his kingdom.

in ancient Egypt as well as the prized hunting dogs of many African tribes. While other dog breeds claim to be the larger hounds depicted in the art of the Pharaohs, new DNA research shows that Pharaoh hounds and Ibizan hounds, often called the oldest of breeds, are really recent constructions. Their appearance matches ancient images but their genes do not.

Basenjis, however, can lay claim to the smaller curlier-tailed hunters in Egyptian art since they were around at the time of the Pharaohs. While researchers still can't agree on the exact time the dog split off from its ancestor the wolf, mitochrondrial DNA evidence places the split in a range from 15,000 to 135,000 years ago. The African Basenji dates very close to the split, which places it in the ancient group. This ancient group includes geographically diverse

TIP

The Double Suspension Gallop

✔ In a normal gallop the body is being catapulted over a leg that is in contact with the ground, and one foot is always on the ground. Sighthounds, and some other galloping breeds, employ the double suspension gallop where they are flying through the air having no contact with the ground.

✔ One suspension phase occurs when the Basenji is fully extended with no feet touching the ground.

✔ The other moment of suspension occurs when the body is contracted with all legs underneath but no feet touching the ground. In the suspended phases, the momentum from the speed carries the body forward.

breeds that are not usually grouped together, including the Chinese Chow-Chow, Shar-Pei, Shih-Tzu, and Pekingese; the Japanese Akita and Shiba Inu; the central African Basenji; the Middle Eastern Saluki and Afghan; and the Tibetan Terrier and Lhasa Apso. Also in that subset are the Nordic breeds including the Arctic Alaskan Malamute, Siberian Husky, and Samoyed. These all have close genetic relationships to the wolf according to recent research.

The Basenji Rediscovered

After the Egyptian era the Basenji lay tucked away in the heart of Africa unknown to the outside world until the early nineteenth century when the breed was rediscovered by British explorers around the headwaters of the Nile and Congo Rivers. These early explorers described the native dogs as small, fawn-colored, and sleek-coated with curly tails. It was also noted that they had prick ears on foxy heads and they did not bark.

Always living in close association with man, the Basenji was prized by the Congo natives for its hunting abilities. Small family groups of Basenjis lived in villages with the Congo (now Zaire) tribes and were free to come and go as they pleased. There were no breeding programs and the Basenjis usually interbred with other dogs in the village. The distance between villages kept the gene pools isolated and pure within each area.

Each village had its own Basenji family and when the dogs followed visiting tribesmen to another village, the Basenjis, respecting the

Basenjis survived for many generations in the African bush.

The first Basenji colors to come out of Africa were reds and tricolors. These original colors were the only ones in the Bar Harbor studies.

other pack's territory, would wait outside the village until their humans returned. In some remote places in Africa the Basenjis still live this way although domestic breeds have infiltrated the continent and marred the purity of the Basenjis in most places.

The Basenji as a Native Hunting Dog

Forest Areas

The hunting style of the Basenji varies with the terrain. When hunting in the forest areas, natives string out nets. The Basenjis work through the brush and drive the game into the nets where the natives can spear the stranded animals. Because the Basenji is a silent hunter—it does not bark—the natives attach bells or rattles to the dogs' necks or waists. This serves to tell the hunter where the dogs are and also to startle the game and get it running toward the net.

Steppe Grass

When hunting in the high steppe grass the Basenjis also wear bells around their neck so the hunters can keep track of them. Being a very agile dog, the Basenji will leap high into the air in order to see the game over the tall grass. In these areas they are known as M'bwa M'Kubwa M'bwa, which translates to the jumping up and down dogs.

Large or Small Animals

Basenjis can hold large animals at bay until the hunters arrive. They are also capable of running down and catching small animals. They have incredible hunting instincts and use all their faculties, sight, scent, and hearing, to get the job done.

Whether hunting alone, as a pack or with their humans, endurance is of great importance to the Basenji. At times many miles must be covered just to get to the hunting grounds. This is where the Basenji's effortless floating

"Goodbye, My Lady" by James Street

The story of a boy who found a lost Basenji in the swamp near his home was first published in 1941 in *The Saturday Evening Post* under the title, *Weep No More, My Lady*. The boy reaches maturity through his experiences with, and eventual loss of, his beloved Lady. In 1954 the story was published in book form and titled *Goodbye, My Lady*. The book was made into a black-and-white movie of the same name in 1956. The Warner Studios' production starred child actor, Brandon de Wilde, Walter Brennan, Phil Harris, and a number of different Basenjis that played the part of Lady. In 1993 *Goodbye, My Lady* was released on video.

After *Weep No More, My Lady* appeared in *The Post* there was such a response of outrage against the boy being separated from his dog that James Street was compelled to write a sequel. *Please Come Home, My Lady*, a lesser-known work, was printed in *The Post* in 1942. A version of this story was printed in the book *Teenage Dog Stories*, published by Grosset and Dunlap. Unfortunately, the sequel never made it to the screen.

Out of Africa

Attempts to bring the Basenji to England began as early as 1895 when they were exhibited at the Cruft's show as African Bush Dogs or Congo Terriers. Unfortunately, these dogs died of distemper shortly after the show.

In 1923 six more Basenji were imported to England. They were placed in quarantine and given distemper inoculations that were in the experimental stage at that time. Tragically, the dogs became ill and died from the aftereffects of the injections.

Most early attempts failed because the Basenjis had no immunity to the viral infections of this foreign land. In 1936 some Basenjis successfully passed through quarantine and in 1937 several more were brought over from Africa. The Basenjis made quite an impact when exhibited at the Cruft's show that year.

By 1959 a significant contribution to the Basenji gene pool came in the form of the little red-and-white female, Fula of the Congo. Veronica Tudor-Williams, who had preserved the Basenji breed through the war years (World War II), ventured into deepest Africa to bring back much-needed new blood to England and ultimately to the rest of the world.

Imports

Early Imports to America

During the 1930s and 1940s Basenjis were arriving in the United States and Canada. In 1941 some of these arrived directly from Africa. Congo, a half-starved, mostly white Basenji, stowed away on a ship loaded with coffee; Kindu and Kasenyi arrived with a shipment of gorillas.

trot serves him well. Once arriving at the hunt he will have to turn on his fast double suspension gallop to run down the game. After several hours of hunting, the Basenji must still have the endurance to get back home before the leopards come out.

Africans often carried their Basenjis to and from the hunt on their shoulders in the manner seen in this photo.

Starting in 1937 Basenji imports came from England to the United States and Canada. In 1942 the Basenji Club of America (BCOA) was formed, and in 1943 Basenjis became eligible for registration with the American Kennel Club (AKC).

Registrations increased slowly in the beginning and the breed remained in the hands of dedicated breeders. The first boost to popularity came in 1950 with the release of the movie, *Goodbye, My Lady*, that was about a lost Basenji. Many people who later acquired a Basenji were first intrigued by the breed when they saw this film.

Popularity

Basenjis remained fairly far down on the popularity list of AKC-registered breeds so have not had to face many of the problems that have appeared in other more popular breeds. Basenjis are not very appealing to the commercial kennels that mass-produce puppies for profit because of their once-a-year breeding cycle. Puppy-millers and backyard breeders quickly learn that Basenjis are not the easiest breed to house because of their ability to escape and their chewing when bored. Because of these things and their other unique traits that make them a dog that is not for everyone, the market for Basenjis is not as readily available as one might think.

A threat to the purity of the native breed in its home country was realized as early as 1945. An expert on Basenjis at that time, Major Tiger

The black-and-white color in Basenjis was brought to the United States in the 1970s.

Wyld, from Yambro, South Sudan, wrote to the British administrator asking for legislation that would stop people from bringing other dogs into the area; this area was considered the country of the barkless dog.

Imports in the 1970s

In 1924 the Firestone Plantations Company, covering about a million acres, was established in Liberia. During the following decades several of the Firestone employees became interested in the native hunting dogs and began breeding them. The natives, however, liked to crossbreed their native dogs with the bigger barking dogs brought in from the outside world. When one worker, Dr. Standifer, returned home to the United States he brought a black-and-white female back with him. This was Kiki of Cryon who was bred to a registered Basenji, Gunn's Ramses. This mating, which produced Black Diamond of Cryon, was whelped June 14, 1962. Black Diamond was acquired by Khajah Kennels where she produced a litter.

Since Kiki was not registered with any kennel club, Black Diamond and her offspring could not be registered with the AKC even though the black-and-white color was already in the breed standard.

Two black males from this litter were sent to England where they were mated with registered English Basenjis for three generations. The next generation was eligible for registration with the Kennel Club in England, and thereafter with the AKC.

As a result of this cooperative venture, a black male, Ch. Sir Datar of Horsley, was returned to Khajah Kennels in 1969. Although some of his siblings and other black-and-white relatives came to this country, Datar is responsible for the majority of the black-and-whites in this country today.

A few other African black-and-white Basenjis from Liberia found their way into the AKC stud books by being first registered with the South African Kennel Club and the Kennel Club of England. Thus, the decade of 1970 brought new blood and the addition of the black-and-white color to the Basenji breed. Prior to this the only two colors in the United States were red-and-white and tricolor.

Imports in the 1980s

The earliest history of the Basenji recorded in cave drawings and Egyptian tombs depicted the dogs as red or black, sometimes with white markings. This was logical as the only colors associated with wild canines are tan (or brown) and black. Early cave drawings showed stripes on tigers and zebras but not on dogs. Written reports from the late 1800s and early 1900s of dogs in Africa also list the colors as some description of red, tan, fawn, or yellow, and, more rarely, as black, some with tan markings.

It wasn't until the mid-1900s that there was any mention of stripes on Basenjis. Veronica Tudor-Williams first wrote of seeing them on her 1959 expedition to Africa when she

Bar Harbor Studies

Basenjis were one of the breeds used by J. P. Scott and J. L. Fuller in their Bar Harbor studies that began in 1946. These studies compared the biological aspects, performance, social behavior, and reactions to stress in five different breeds. A social hierarchy was apparent in the Basenjis. There were two color patterns of Basenjis at this time—red and white and black, tan, and white (referred to as tricolors).

The project began in 1946 and involved five breeds of purebred dogs—the American Cocker Spaniel, Basenji, Beagle, Shetland Sheepdog, and Wire Fox Terrier. One of the reasons the Basenji was chosen was because it was closest to the wild type among the domestic breeds.

Social hierarchy: J. P. Scott and J. L. Fuller note that the social hierarchy in Basenjis was more apparent than in the Cockers. In tests with a maze the Basenjis were confident and scored well but were poorly motivated.

Barking: Scott compared barking behavior between Basenjis and Cockers under stress. While Cockers tended to continue high-pitched yaps for dozens or even hundreds of times, Basenjis managed only a low woof with much effort and gave up after two or three barks. Crossing and backcrossing the two breeds suggested that barking or not barking under social stress was due to genes having the effect of altering the threshold of response.

Tasks: Fuller found Basenjis tended to do best in tasks requiring independent action and were poor in those depending on responsiveness to a handler.

A nicely marked black, tan, and white Basenji. This color pattern is also referred to as tricolor.

brought Fula back to England. A brindle male puppy was also acquired on this expedition but Miss Tudor-Williams chose to keep Fula instead of Tiger, as he was named, because the Basenji Club of Great Britain stated that members must not breed creams or brindles. Tiger went to Southern Rhodesia where he sired a litter and his descendants (non-brindle) went to England and later to the United States, but the brindle color was not established at this time.

Health: By the 1980s the most serious of the Basenjis' health problems had become devastating. Fanconi Syndrome (see page 75), a dysfunction of the renal tubules of the kidney, was taking its toll on the Basenji population and was thought to be inherited because of the high incidence in the breed.

Some of the breeders that were hardest hit felt that adding new genes to the gene pool was the only way to save the breed. Using health improvement as their main justification, they managed to convince the American Kennel Club to open the stud books to unregistered native African dogs with no pedigrees.

Expeditions were made in 1987 and 1988 to central Africa in an attempt to salvage some remaining Basenji genes to be used to expand the Basenji gene pool in the United States. Many of the dogs brought back from these expeditions were brindle so the Basenji Club of America changed the Basenji standard to include this new color.

These new dogs and their descendants are identified in the gene pool by the use of the pre-fix *Avongara*, which seems to have been the only restriction put on the use of these new imports. A few breeders have chosen to keep the new Africans pure, but for the most part the new stock was bred randomly into the existing gene pool in an effort to improve health in the breed.

A decade and a half and many generations down the road breeders are seeing that the magic bullet missed its target and the breed still faces the same inherited health problems that were present prior to the Avongara imports. Research is being renewed to search for an inherited component in the genes.

Color: One other import was accepted into the stud book while it was open. This was a red-and-white female Basenji named Esenjo. Esenjo was brought from Zaire in August of 1978. Margaret Sommer of California carried on a controlled breeding program with Esenjo who was bred to one of her AKC-registered domestic males. When the stud books were opened this family of Basenjis was accepted for registration along with the Avongaras. Unfortunately, only a few Esenjo descendants are in the gene pool today.

More Recent Imports from Africa

The beginning of this century finds some interested Basenji fanciers bringing in some African native dogs from a remote and isolated part of Benin (western Africa—deeper into the continent than Liberia). The little dogs, called *Avuvi* in the native dialect, are homogenous (uniform in type and genetic makeup) and very much in keeping with the Basenji standard (see Selecting Your Basenji—What to Look for in Your Basenji). The Avuvi dogs that are already in this country have been DNA-tested for iden-tification and parentage. Further DNA testing is being done on other dogs in the villages where they came from and a photographic record of these native dogs is being kept.

The interested breeders will be breeding the Avuvis in a planned and controlled pro-gram where testing will be continued. At this point, the dogs in the project will only be bred within the project. Unlike the last imports, these dogs will not be turned loose into the gene pool until test breeding has been done and health and other factors have been determined.

While it is not likely that the AKC will ever open the Basenji stud books again, they do consider registrations on a case-by-case basis. The Avuvis can be registered with other kennel clubs and gain AKC registration the same as the early black-and-white Basenjis did. One Avuvi Basenji, registered with the United Ken-nel Club, has already gained her UKC champi-onship. The history of these Avuvi Basenjis is currently being written.

Basenjis often lay with their paws crossed.

*Basenjis will
invent their own
games; here they
have invented
the "hat chase."*

*This Basenji
puppy is
surveying his
one-acre fenced
yard.*

UNDERSTANDING YOUR BASENJI

The Basenji has been out of his native jungle for less than a century compared to most other canines that have lived in civilization for many hundreds of years. Even though the Basenjis lived with humans in Africa, they were not owned or controlled by them. There were no leashes or fences or closed doors; Basenjis lived in harmony with their humans.

Making the Adjustment

Basenjis, having been hunters that depended on the kill for food, have developed as independent thinkers rather than subservient working dogs that take direction easily. In their native land they lived among the tribesmen but were free to come and go at will. Basenjis sometimes display an aloof attitude toward people, especially strangers, but they do form a strong bond with family and friends.

Imagine the adjustments these free-spirited little dogs have made to come live with us in a civilized, overcrowded, and controlling society. In today's fast-paced world it is not safe to let a Basenji wander at will and fend for himself—

Be sure that there are no plants in your yard, such as iris bulbs, that are poisonous to dogs.

motor vehicles are the number one killer of Basenjis. Basenjis have no fear of them and are likely to dart out in front of one.

Basenjis have to be confined and deep down in their ancestral essence there is a resentment and resistance to this. Instinct makes them escape artists and more than one has been appropriately named Houdini. We, as their guardians, must make confinement as acceptable as possible for them. The best way to do this is with proper training from day one (see Training Your Basenji, page 61).

The Pack Mentality

The Basenji is a "pack animal" that does best when living in a structured society. Civilization has changed the makeup of his pack because he can no longer roam free with his relatives. Today his "pack" consists of his human family.

Basenjis can climb out of an X-pen like this one. It is best to have a top; but, even then, keep an eye on them.

The Basenji's instinctive need for hierarchy is still strong and every pack must have a leader. If you are not that loved and respected leader, your Basenji will be glad to take over the position. This is not an acceptable situation. Basenjis have been known to control households and this usually leads to their people being forced to give up the dog to a rescue organization or worse. However, the Basenji, once having been allowed to learn all the wrong things in life, may or may not be a candidate for rehabilitation.

When properly bred and raised, a Basenji will become a loyal and loving companion, but it is important that he learn his position in the pack. When his position is clear and unchanging he will accept this and feel secure when he has a strong leader. There are books that tell how to dominate your pets but animals are not fooled by false pretenses. The "alpha leader"

idea has been overdone and misrepresented in many books on training and does not work well with the Basenji. If you are not an alpha person by nature, don't try to pretend that you are; your Basenji will see right through you. You need not be a drill sergeant or a bully but you do need to be in charge.

Punishment: Basenjis do not respond well to punishment or harsh treatment. This is not a breed that will tolerate being abused; they will retaliate and get back at you by being destructive or by urinating on something with your scent on it. Basenjis will sulk when they feel they have been treated unfairly.

The more modern methods of training by reward and praise rather than punishment work the best with Basenjis. They are not dogs of slave mentality. Only fair and consistent treatment, along with love and understanding, will make one your friend for life.

Attributes

A Sense of Humor

Basenjis have many unique qualities; one is a sense of humor. They like to tease each other or any member of their pack, including you. Once they find a behavior that annoys you they will persist in doing it until you reach your breaking point. They always know just how far to push a person and when reaching that point they will stop, look you in the eye, and yodel. You need to have an equally good sense of humor to live with a Basenji.

Heatseekers

Basenjis are sun worshipers; they love to sleep in a sunny spot. If sunshine is not available, a spot close to a fireplace or heat vent is their next choice unless they can snuggle up close to a warm human. They like to be covered with a blanket. They also enjoy a warm coat or sweater in the winter. It is rarely too hot for a Basenji and you know it is a very hot day if your Basenji pants. This is a clean breed that does not drool. Basenjis also drink less water than other dogs of the same size even in hot weather.

A Mind of Their Own

Basenjis can be single-minded and unbelievably persistent when they want to do something. If you have taught them *"No"* they will stop doing whatever you correct them for and then go right back to it. You can keep saying, *"No,"* and continue their game or you can take the object away from the dog or the dog away from the object. This persistence can also be a good thing when channeled in the right direction.

Catlike

Basenjis are catlike in personality:
✔ They will wash themselves.
✔ They like to sit in high places.
✔ They do not like to get their feet wet. One of the most challenging things about living with a Basenji is getting him to go outside to relieve himself when it is raining or the ground is wet.

The Energetic Basenji

Basenjis need a lot of exercise, especially when they are young. Basenji puppies have an incredible amount of energy. The best way to "burn it off" is to have a securely fenced area

Basenjis are heat seekers and like to be warm. This one sports his winter coat.

where the Basenji can run at will. Just being outside in the fresh air and sunshine will help wear down an exuberant Basenji puppy. Investigating different parts of the yard will help fulfill his need for mental exercise as well as his physical need to move around.

An older Basenji will not run a lot if alone in a yard. The only way an older dog will exercise hard is if he can see something that excites him, such as another dog or cat passing by.

Jogging with the dog on lead helps but is not as good as having a fenced yard. Throwing a ball for the Basenji to retrieve may work for a little while but most Basenjis become bored with this quickly. That thinking Basenji brain will soon decide that if you keep throwing it away, you can just go get it yourself!

Although they have a lot of energy, the Basenji is not a hyperactive dog. He will be happy to lie quietly next to you for hours while

Basenjis are friendly dogs as long as they are with their own pack, but most are not so friendly with strange Basenjis.

you watch TV or sleep as long as he has had his exercise.

The Barkless Dog

Everyone knows that Basenjis are barkless, but few are prepared for the noises they *can* make. An unhappy Basenji can howl and scream with ear-piercing sounds that carry for long distances. Many an unsuspecting apartment dweller has made this discovery too late to save their dog or home. Many owners have become governed by a smart Basenji that has learned to get his way and be let out of his crate by throwing a tantrum that has to be silenced before the neighbors complain. The only way to prevent this is by correct early crate-training (see page 45) and you only get one chance to do it right the first time.

In spite of being barkless, Basenjis make good watchdogs. Nothing goes unnoticed. If something is different from the norm your Basenji will be aware of it. Their keen hearing will let them know of someone approaching well in advance of a human noticing anything unusual. Instead of barking, a Basenji reacts to stress by running. If loose, he will run to you and back to whatever is amiss. If he is crated he will be on his feet and alert; you will hear him circling excitedly in the crate.

Cause

Autopsies have shown that the Basenji has physical structures that differ from other dogs. His more shallow laryngeal ventricle and reduced laryngeal saccule probably contribute to his inability to bark effortlessly. Different physical structure coupled with his higher stress tolerance have made the Basenji a barkless dog.

What You Can Expect

Living with a Basenji is like living with a perpetual two-year-old child who has a very high IQ. They need to have their brains stimulated and their curiosity satisfied. When you are not on hand to provide entertainment and guidance, Basenjis need to be confined in an escape-proof area where there is nothing they can hurt or be hurt by. This is why responsible Basenji breeders strongly suggest the use of a crate inside the home and a securely fenced area outside. What to look out for:

✔ The only good Basenji is a tired Basenji! There is a certain amount of energy that Basenjis must burn up every day, especially when they are puppies. Basenjis are perpetual puppies; they remain playful into old age. The more energy they expend outdoors, the less they will expend in the house.

✔ The inquisitiveness and persistence of this breed will come as a surprise to most people. You will have a constant companion and *helper* when working around the house or yard; there will be a little nose investigating everything you do. They will even carry your tools—but usually in the wrong direction. They have no fear so it is best to put them in their crate if you are running a lawn mower or anything else that could be dangerous to a curious Basenji.

✔ Food on the table or on a counter is not safe if you turn your back for a second. It is wise to put your Basenji out in his yard or in his crate when it is your mealtime.

✔ Basenjis will get into your trash every chance they get. Most Basenji owners keep their trash cans behind closed doors (fastened shut) or in high places.

✔ Tissues of any sort are fair game and your Basenji may come running out of the bath-room with a whole roll streaming behind him. Keep the roll up high or keep the door closed. To a Basenji, soft fuzzy things are the same as fur and feather and must be destroyed. It's the breed's nature.

✔ Another great sport for Basenjis is rolling on damp towels or dirty clothes. If your Basenji is there when you step out of the shower, he will insist on drying you.

Interacting with Humans

Basenji puppies should be friendly with every-one but as they get older they get selective. Their family is their pack and friends of the family who visit often will be your Basenji's friends too. With strangers the adult Basenji may be more aloof. When meeting a Basenji for the first time

Basenjis are hams and like to show off. They can provide a little extra entertainment— even in the conformation ring.

a person should always let the Basenji make the first advances. If a person forces himself or her-self on a Basenji, the dog will resent it and may even go so far as to snap. Basenjis consider a certain area around them to be their personal space and it is best not to invade it. This applies to humans and other animals. On the other hand, it is best not to allow your Basenji to be the one that is rude and invades another dog's private space. Either way, a fight can break out especially if the dogs are both Basenjis.

Intelligence

The uncanny intelligence of this breed is a mixed blessing. For those who understand and love the breed it is an endless joy to have a

Basenjis share secrets and impart wisdom to the younger generations.

learning all you can about this breed. Remember that the puppy begins learning when he is born and everything he experiences in the first few months of life will set the mold forever. This is why it is important to buy your puppy from a responsible, knowledgeable breeder who will see that both the puppy and you get off to the right start. Mistakes made at an early age are hard, if not impossible, to eradicate.

Idiosyncrasies of the Breed

Basenjis have many strange mannerisms and are often referred to as catlike.

✔ They like to be up high and prefer lying on the back of a sofa to lying on the seat.

✔ They sleep in strange positions and will lie on their backs with their legs up and their head and neck turned to the side for balance. Often you will find one sleeping with his head, neck, shoulders, and front legs dangling precariously off the side of a chair or sofa, and you will wonder why he doesn't slide off.

✔ When your Basenji is unhappy with you he has his way of letting you know it. He will sit up very straight and stiff like a cat statue with his back toward you, then he will glance back over his shoulder to see if you are aware that you are being ignored.

✔ While sitting in this position they can also put their head up and look straight back and can swivel their head around in a 360-degree circle. New owners will be surprised when they repeat this action several times to get attention.

✔ Basenjis are very aware of "up" and will watch a bird or airplane flying overhead.

four-legged companion that is so responsive, creative, and entertaining. On the other hand, if you are not prepared for this kind of brainpower in a dog you may be caught defenseless and become frustrated. Basenjis can combine all the tricks that all the other breeds have thought up plus many original games of their own. This is not to say they can't be dealt with, but you will need to have two things on your side: you must be smarter than they are and you must have a good sense of humor.

Chewing

Like any puppy, Basenjis chew and take it to a high degree of perfection. They chew to get out, they chew to get in, they chew to get loose, and they chew to chew. Usually they chew because they are bored. They need to be given appropriate things to chew on, especially when they are teething. They need to be trained that there are many things they must not chew.

Life with a Basenji can be interesting, challenging, and rewarding. The secret to success is

Basenji play can be rough at times, like this attack from above.

✔ Basenjis will bow down in front to entice you or another animal to play. If that doesn't work, they will take their paws and cover their eyes or draw their paws down over their face. Or they will look up at you and give out an enticing yodel that will make you melt.

Basenjis have many endearing qualities but still are not for everyone and they don't try to be! But for those people who understand and love the breed there can be no other. Once you truly *know* a Basenji, every other dog is just a dog!

IS A BASENJI THE RIGHT DOG FOR YOU?

You may desire a Basenji for many reasons: they are attractive, medium-sized, and short-coated. They wash themselves like a cat, are quiet most of the time, travel well, and are intelligent. They don't drool and don't have long sweeping tails to knock things off coffee tables or beat your leg. However, Basenjis are not a breed for everyone and there are many things to consider in deciding if a Basenji is right for you.

How to Decide If a Basenji Is Right for You

Take a piece of paper and make a list of the things that you want to get from owning a dog in one column and a list of things that you don't want to live with in a dog in another column. While studying the information in this book put a checkmark beside the items you have listed in your columns. No breed is perfect but you want to acquire the one that best fits you and your lifestyle. By listing the pros and cons you can look at the overall picture and determine what compromises you are willing to make.

Basenjis sit up straight like cat statues, and will sometimes rock back with their tails under them and their back legs sticking out past the front legs.

Things to Consider

A Basenji needs to have his inquisitiveness, inventiveness, and sense of adventure fulfilled. If you cannot provide this for your Basenji he will find a way to entertain himself; chances are you will not like what he finds.

Anyone with a demanding and domineering personality should probably not have a Basenji. This is not a dog that will accept unfair domination so if you want something to inflict your will upon, a Basenji is not for you. Anyone who takes himself too seriously should not have a Basenji; if you can't laugh at yourself, a Basenji is not for you.

If you want your Basenji to be more than just a companion, he can oblige. Many Basenjis are successful show dogs. Basenjis like to lure course. This is a pleasant way to spend time in the great outdoors while letting your Basenji

Older children and puppies are great together.

consider. Purchasing a dog is not like buying a commodity. This is a flesh and blood living creature that you are taking on as your responsibility. You cannot just throw him out or trade him in when you have become tired of him or if he no longer performs as you would like or if he gets old. Taking on a Basenji is a 12- to 15-year (or more) commitment. Are you prepared for that?

A Basenji that has lived for many years with the people he loves does not usually adjust to a new home in his old age. You need to be willing and able to stand by your pet in his senior years and not dump him because your lifestyle has changed and he is now viewed as a burden. Euthanasia is far kinder if you *must* get rid of your pet.

A dog needs proper nutrition, a veterinarian's care, exercise, and training. The upkeep can be time-consuming and costly. Are you ready for this responsibility in your life?

Is the Timing Right?

You must also ask yourself if this is the right time to get a Basenji. The answer to this depends on your current situation in life and what you expect to be doing over the next decade or two. For example, young families decide to get a dog to "grow up with the kids." Here timing is the all-important factor that will determine if this can be done successfully or not.

Bringing home a puppy creates a lot of work that, sooner or later, falls on the mother or caregiver. Today's lifestyle usually requires that

work off some energy. Performance events such as agility and obedience take a lot more skill on the owner's part but your Basenji will be up to it if you are (see Special Activities for You and Your Basenji, page 83).

A Commitment for the Life of the Dog

Owning a dog is not all glitter and glory; there are commitments and responsibilities to

These adorable puppies will soon become adults and can be expected to live well into their teens. Getting a dog is a commitment for the life of the dog.

both parents work and a young puppy must eat three or four times a day and eliminate at least twice that often, not to mention his other needs. Will someone be home to look after these chores? We can't just turn Fido loose to run over a 200-acre farm anymore.

The Average Family

Let's take a scenario of an average family where the children are very young and the mother (or baby-sitter) is home with them. Young Jane just started school; David will start kindergarten soon, and baby Jimmy is starting to stand—"Let's get a puppy!"

A breed rescuer got a call from the mother of just such a family. The husband/father (at work all day) wanted a dog and brought home a Basenji puppy. What fun! Well, for a few days anyway. The mother told of her frustrating experiences of trying to cope with training a puppy, driving the oldest to and from school, getting the middle child (barely toilet-trained) ready for kindergarten, and the baby, still in diapers, needing constant attention. Add to this the housework, shopping, cooking, husband's demands, and such, and you have one tired mom. She told the rescue lady that today was the last straw. She was tired of hearing the baby cry all the time because the puppy had run off with his toys. She was late for picking up the oldest at school; the middle child had fallen and hurt himself. While she had been changing the baby the puppy had grabbed the dirty diaper and run off with it, strewing the

contents all through the house she had just cleaned. The Basenji had to go! "If you can't help," sobbed the woman, "I'll have to take her to the pound."

Stress on the Caregiver

In considering the right time to get a puppy, be sure to take into account the stress that will be placed on the caregiver. There are other things to consider where puppies and babies are concerned: Crawling babies and toddlers share the same floor with the puppy and puppies tend to steal the babies' toys. Puppies mature faster than babies, are steadier on their feet, and capable of bowling over a toddler with a slight bump. Young dogs view toddlers and young children as people-puppies and tend to play with them accordingly.

Puppies play by chewing on each other. But teething on baby's arm is not a good idea. A baby's skin is soft and tender and the puppy's teeth and nails are very sharp. When Junior ends up with cuts and scratches, the puppy will

Young children and puppies should be supervised. Children need to be gentle with Basenjis.

if someone will have the time to dedicate to this. A puppy *home alone* can get into all kinds of mischief, some of which can be fatal to the dog as well as destructive to the home. Unsupervised, a puppy will develop bad habits.

One good time to acquire a puppy is a year or more *before* the first child arrives, then the dog can be properly raised and trained before there are children. When properly introduced, such a dog will be good with babies and small children and not put as much stress on the family. If the children arrive first, then the youngest child should be old enough to understand and respect animals. Puppies are great for older children (six and up) and can teach them a sense of responsibility. But one or the other, child or dog, must be mature enough to understand and respect the ways of the other. Timing is everything. If you have children already, getting a puppy is like throwing another child that is a fast, strong, two-year-old genius into the mix. Ask yourself if you are prepared to cope with that at this time.

This is not to say that not everyone can cope with puppies and babies at the same time. Many people do, but usually they are animal-oriented to begin with and understand the nature of the beasts because they have grown up with animals. So you must look at the makeup and experience of your household. Don't forget about relatives and neighbors who visit you; you must consider them as extended family.

Dogs make great family pets under the right circumstances, and every child should have a dog at some time in his or her life—but make

probably get blamed and sometimes branded as vicious.

Puppy teeth are like needles, but when the puppy is older and the second teeth have come in, they are bigger and blunter and not as apt to scratch tender skin. Also, an older dog will have better sense about how to use his mouth. When dogs are young, they want to mouth everything.

Very young children tend to run and scream in high-pitched voices. In some dogs this can trigger the *prey instinct* and they will attack. This is one of the reasons why many small children are badly bitten by dogs every year. Bad experiences in childhood can traumatize an individual for life.

When Is a Good Time to Get a Basenji Puppy?

As discussed earlier, one must look at the time involved in raising a puppy and determine

Training is done at many different levels. Basenjis should be exposed to many different things at a young age.

sure the timing is right. Pair puppies with older children. Adult dogs should get along with all ages if they are properly socialized with children from the time they are puppies.

When Is a Bad Time to Get a Basenji Puppy?

"Let's get a puppy for Christmas!"

Whoa! Let's *think* about this! Is it wise to bring home a puppy at a busy time like the holidays? The vision of a puppy under the tree on Christmas morning is great for artists, but let's get real! Picture the Christmas tree prone on the floor and the gifts in shreds because you were too busy making dinner to watch the puppy. Picture a puppy that has swallowed a battery or choked on tinsel and has to be rushed to the veterinarian.

With all the hustle and bustle of Christmas do you really have time to exercise a puppy every two hours 24/7 at this most crucial training time in a puppy's life? This would not be fair to the puppy or to you.

Pick a quieter time of year to get a puppy when there is nothing else going on to take all your time and energy. Timing is important in raising a Basenji puppy that will be a good canine citizen. It will be stressful enough for a puppy going into a new home. He does not need the extra stress of company and holiday activities until he has had time to adjust to his new surroundings.

They hate rain and wet ground and will take care of business much faster on a dry spot such as dry leaves or grass.

There are occasional litters born at other times of the year but these are rare and hard to find. The best selection of puppies will be at the normal breeding season. Keep this in mind when choosing a Basenji to be your canine friend. Most responsible breeders have waiting lists for their puppies before they breed. To be assured of getting a good puppy it is wise to get on the waiting list of such a breeder.

Fortunately, most Basenjis are born at a time when they are not old enough to go for Christmas presents. A responsible Basenji breeder will be willing to hold any puppies that may be born early in the season until after the holidays.

Basenji Puppies Are Not Available Year Round

The time of year can have a bearing on whether or not one should be getting a Basenji puppy. Basenjis, unlike other domestic dogs, have only one breeding cycle a year. It is in the fall, with puppies being born around the holidays and ready to go to new homes eight or more weeks later (usually January through March). If you live in a section of the country that has cold winters, be prepared for the added difficulty this will cause in house-training a puppy. Shivering outside in the cold will not hurry things along. Basenjis love a good romp in the snow as long as it is not too long.

Puppy or Young Adult?

Raising a puppy is very time-consuming and takes a lot of work. If you do not have the time and patience to devote to doing a good job, perhaps you should consider getting an older Basenji. Finding a properly raised young adult is not easy but it is possible. Responsible breeders take back the dogs they have produced if the owners have to give them up. Also, a breeder may raise a puppy that does not measure up to show potential. When dogs such as these become available, they are a golden opportunity for a working person who does not have time to do a puppy justice.

A Golden Opportunity Dog

This is one that has been well bred and sold into a home where it was properly raised with help from the breeder. These are cherished pets that are given up only because of unforeseen conditions such as illness, death, divorce, relocation, or other unfortunate events.

Older Basenjis have had lots of experiences in life—some were good and some were bad.

A Basenji puppy retrieving a frisbee. Puppies can be fun but they take a lot of work.

Rescues

There are also rescues that are up for adoption. Here you are gambling on what you may get. Sometimes there are good ones, usually given up for legitimate reasons, but mostly they have lost their homes because they were not raised and trained properly and developed into something the owners couldn't live with. Some of these can be rehabilitated but it is a long slow process and should not be undertaken by amateurs. It's like getting a used car—rescues come with all the past owner's problems. But don't rule one out. Many a good dog has been trapped in a bad situation.

Your Basenji Is a Pet!

Single or young married people often make a common but serious mistake when getting a Basenji puppy or adult. They treat him as though he is their spoiled child, allowing the Basenji to run the household by catering to his every demand. What happens when another person is added to this household and finds a Basenji in charge? What happens when a baby is on the way and the parents are afraid the dog will resent the baby and maybe harm it? Then this monster of their own creation has to go, and ends up in rescue or worse.

Remember that you are getting a Basenji for a *pet* and treat it that way. Yes, he is part of your family and your responsibility but he is not the breadwinner, he is not the boss, he is not the baby; he is the family pet and must learn his place in the hierarchy as such.

If there are only adults in the household or if you live alone, things are less complicated but you must still remain the leader of the pack. Be sure that you have adequate time to give to caring for, training, and socializing your Basenji.

SELECTING YOUR BASENJI

Now that you feel a Basenji is the right breed for you, the next step is finding the right individual. A good-quality Basenji at a reasonable price that will have good temperament and health can best be found by going to a responsible, knowledgeable breeder. You should purchase your Basenji from someone who will guide you and be there to answer questions after the sale.

Where to Start

"Buy from a breeder" is the advice given to those seeking a purebred dog but what does it mean? Isn't anyone who breeds a litter of puppies a breeder? Unfortunately, the answer to that is "yes." Since there are all kinds of breeders, how do you select the right one?

Since early experiences affect a dog for life you want to be sure to buy from breeders who have raised their puppies carefully from birth. It is important that a puppy have the care, warmth, and socialization of his mother and littermates in his first few weeks of life. He also needs individual handling and loving care from his breeder in order to accept people as part of his world.

A typical male Basenji with a far-seeing expression on his face.

Puppies need to have space to crawl away from the nest when they need to eliminate; this is the beginning of house-training. Puppies that are raised *en masse* for profit do not have this opportunity. By necessity they learn to sleep in their filth instead of learning to be clean, so they are difficult, if not impossible, to house-train when they are older.

In order for a dog to know that he is a dog and to be able to socialize with other canines it is imperative that he live with his littermates for the first eight weeks of life. He also needs occasional discipline from his mother during this time. At the same time it is important for the puppy to have lots of human contact. A dedicated hobby breeder whose interest is maintaining the breed rather than profiting from it will supply all of this. Puppies raised in quantity for profit do not get a correct start, which leads to problems for the owners later in life.

TIP

A Responsible Basenji Breeder

1. is willing to talk to you about the breed and answer all of your questions.

2. has had a lot of experience with the breed and knows a lot about the line he is using in his breeding program. An inexperienced breeder who knows only slightly more than you do will be of little help, no matter how willing he is to work with you.

3. is willing to show you his dogs and let you meet them close up.

4. asks you a lot of questions. Do not be offended by this—a good breeder wants to know that his puppy will have a good home and that you are the kind of person who will be happy with a Basenji.

5. is willing to take the dog back at any time in its life if, for some unforeseen reason, the purchaser is no longer able to keep it. Responsible breeders do not want their puppies resold, re-homed, or dumped at a shelter or rescue.

6. will be available to you after the sale to make sure everything is going well for you and the puppy.

7. will offer suggestions for feeding, training, and general care of your Basenji.

8. will insist that you have and use an appropriate crate for your dog and will strongly request that you have a securely fenced outside exercise area.

9. will help you select which puppy will best fit into your lifestyle or tell you if you would do better getting an adult dog that has been properly raised and already trained. Take advantage of this person's wealth of knowledge.

10. will tell you all the disadvantages of the breed as well as all the good points. An informed owner will be a longtime, happy owner. Beware of people who say they have perfect dogs or use high-pressure selling tactics.

11. is patient with you. Do not buy from a breeder who is in a hurry to get the puppies out the door. It is very important that a breeder keep the puppies together until they are at least eight weeks old.

12. gives the first shots to the puppies and hopefully keeps them in individual crates for at least a few nights before they go to new homes. Nothing is more important for living with a Basenji than early crate-training.

13. is honest enough to tell you if a Basenji is not right for you. Such a breeder may suggest a more suitable breed for your lifestyle.

14. sells his pets on Limited Registration (offspring cannot be registered) to be spayed/neutered.

15. does not require anything of you other than that you give the dog a good home and possibly do some health testing for inherited breed problems. Most pet owners do not wish to breed and should not be required to breed as a condition of the sale. Beware of "deals" where the seller requires you to breed the Basenji and give puppies back to him. These people are only in it for the money. Dogs sold as pets should not be bred.

16. will stand behind his dogs and if they should develop an inherited disease will offer to replace the dog or make whatever adjustment is appropriate.

A Responsible Basenji Breeder (continued)

17. will want to know if you encounter any health problems or other concerns with your Basenji. Some may require that you have health testing done for some of the late-onset problems in the breed. This is how a breeder tracks possible problems in his line in order to avoid them in the future.

18. has clean facilities and well-cared-for and well-behaved dogs.

19. does not have overcrowded conditions and does not raise more puppies at one time than he can give individual attention to when they are young.

20. will share his knowledge with you and be available to answer your questions as they arise.

Basenjis investigating a sprinkler; they are curious about everything.

Puppy farmers send their poorly bred and raised produce to market at an early age, while they are still cute and cuddly. This traps impulse buyers, who usually end up adding the expense of extra veterinary bills and private training to their already overpriced purchase. Even with the best-intended owners, these dogs may or may not become acceptable pets.

Commercial breeders are in it for the money and sell lesser-quality dogs for higher prices than a responsible hobby breeder or show breeder would charge for a carefully bred, raised, and socialized puppy from a health-tested background. The best way to insure getting a good puppy that you can be proud of is to get on a responsible breeder's waiting list.

Basenjis enjoy traveling with their families. Well-behaved, well-trained Basenjis are a pleasure to take places.

How to Find Responsible Breeders

The best place to start is to contact the national breed club for a list of their members who breed and live in your area. In this case, you want the Basenji Club of America (BCOA), *www.basenji.org*. This site will give you the contact information for the Basenji referral person in your geographical area. The contact person will give you a list of Basenji breeders in your immediate area who are members of the BCOA.

This list is a good starting point as these people are involved with the national club and have had the opportunity to be better educated about the breed than the average non-member. Talk to as many breeders as you can in order to choose one who will work with you. But do not consider this list an endorsement of any kind. You are still on your own to choose the breeder who will best be able to help you.

When you are talking with breeders do not be afraid to ask them for recommendations of other breeders. Tell them exactly what you would like to have in a pet, what facilities you have, how your dog will be cared for, if you have children or not, and what other pets you have. This will enable the breeder to work with you in making decisions. If the breeder is not interested in how his puppies are going to live in their new homes, look for a more caring breeder.

What Purpose Will Your Basenji Serve in Your Life?

The first, and most important, thing that you want in your Basenji is that he be a good companion. He will be your buddy at home and a traveling companion if you want to take him with you to other places. Some owners will want to go further and do more with their dogs such as showing, obedience, agility, lure coursing, hunting, therapy work, or tracking. A Basenji will be up to anything you are capable of; his intended purpose will factor into your decision when selecting your Basenji.

Good Temperament

✔ No matter what the intended purpose, the most important thing to look for in a Basenji is good temperament.

✔ A dog must be sound of mind as well as body.

✔ A Basenji should be stable and adaptable.

A well-bred Basenji is regal and beautiful. This tricolor girl is relaxing in the sun.

✔ As puppies they should all be outgoing and friendly. As a Basenji gets older, he may get more aloof toward strangers but will always consider your family as his pack. He will remember people who visit you frequently but may regard strangers with caution.

Male or Female?

There is only a slight difference in personality between a male and female Basenji. The female can be more independent than the male. The males seem to bond closer and are more willing to obey. Basenji males are not leg lifters as are males of many breeds that are constantly marking. Many young male puppies relieve themselves by squatting; as they get a little bigger they may urinate to the side without lifting a leg. Sometimes they are several years old before they actually lift their leg. Basenji males are not inclined to ride things like a lot of male dogs do.

A first-time Basenji owner may find a male a little easier to live with than a female. Also, when it comes to neutering, the surgery on a male is less invasive.

A lovely female Basenji.

One or Two Basenjis?

Having two adult Basenjis works out really well. They are good company for each other *but* it is not advisable to get two puppies at the same time. Every puppy deserves to be an only child for a little while in its life.

> Double your pleasure, double your fun
> But don't get two 'till you can control one!

1. Training one puppy is difficult enough but two at one time will more than double your problems.

2. If there are two you will never know for sure which one made the mess.

3. Two Basenji puppies will influence each other into being naughty.

4. Puppies have different personalities and one may need a firm hand and loud voice while another may be overwhelmed by harsh discipline.

5. Two at once will bond to each other and not as well to you. Each puppy should have his own time to bond with his human counterpart.

Dogs learn from each other. Get one Basenji puppy at a time. Train the first one properly because the second one will learn from him. This makes it doubly important to have the first one well trained because the second one will copy—especially *bad* habits. A well-trained adult will help you raise the second puppy.

What to Look for in Your Basenji

The most important qualities in a companion are good temperament and personality. If you can't live with the dog, other qualities matter very little. Of course you want a healthy dog and one that looks like its breed. To learn what a breed of dog should look like, refer to the breed's AKC standard. This is the blueprint by which dogs are judged in conformation competition.

The Standard

Each breed of dog that is recognized by the American Kennel Club has a standard of perfection. The AKC describes the standard as follows: "The standard portrays what in the mind of its compilers would be the ideal dog of the breed. Ideal in type, in structure, in gait, in temperament—ideal in every way."

However, it is the breed's National Club, in this case, the Basenji Club of America, that actually determines what the standard shall be and then it is approved by the AKC. Because the Basenji is a natural breed that has evolved through hundreds of years, it is the responsibility of the breed club to preserve this breed in its original form. The breed should not be

A brindle Basenji in a show pose.

changed to suit the whims of man or to follow the fads of the show ring.

The standard describes the Basenji as a small, short-haired hunting dog that hunts by sight and scent. He is lightly built with a short back and appears high on leg compared to his length (square as opposed to rectangular). The Basenji has small, pricked ears, almond eyes, and a wrinkled forehead with side wrinkles greatly desired. His coat is short and shiny and his hide is soft and pliant. His tail is relatively short and high-set, curled close to the body. The Basenji's demeanor is proud, alert, and inquisitive. He is elegant, graceful, and moves freely and efficiently.

Males should look masculine and females should look feminine. The ideal height is 17 inches (43 cm) at the shoulder for males and 16 inches (40.6 cm) for females. The approved colors are red, black-and-tan, black, and brindle, all with white markings. White is required on chest, feet, and tail tip. White blaze, legs, and collar are optional. The white should never predominate over the amount of color, nor should the white break up the solid body color. Colors should be clear and bright with the line of demarcation between the black-and-tan well defined so that the two do not blend causing a muddy color.

You can purchase a brochure from the BCOA Secretary that contains the standard along with pictures and clarifying comments (see Information page for address).

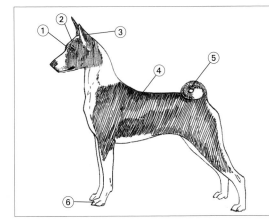

Illustrated Standard

1. Almond-shaped eyes
2. Fine, profuse wrinkles on forehead, visible when ears are erect
3. Small erect ears
4. Short back
5. Tail bends acutely forward and lies well curled over to either side
6. Small oval feet

❏ **Color:** red, black, black and tan, or brindle, all with white feet, chest and tail tips; white legs, blaze, and collar optional
❏ **DQ:** none

RAISING YOUR BASENJI PUPPY

The importance of a puppy's experiences in the first few months of life cannot be overemphasized. This most formative time of a dog's life will make him or break him forever. As soon as you bring your Basenji home, the lessons must begin. Not only will you need to teach him what is acceptable, you will also need to prevent him from learning bad habits—"An ounce of prevention is worth a pound of cure!"

Early Socialization (Canine and Human)

It is important to know what a puppy needs in his earliest life so that you can choose a breeder who has been conscientious about these things. The puppy's parents should be healthy and receiving good nutrition. This is especially important to the dam so that the fetuses develop normally.

The first days of a puppy's life should be spent in the warm, dry company of his mother and littermates. It is important that he be kept warm, for puppies cannot make their own body heat for the first 48 hours. This is also a good time for the removal of the dewclaws. The ear-

A young brindle puppy checking out the fall decorations. Puppies should be introduced to many different things while they are young.

lier it is done, the less scarring there will be. The puppies are aware of touch and of being handled. Gentle handling is good stimulation for the puppy and his first introduction to humans.

The dam will clean the puppies and help them eliminate so there is very little work for the breeder at this point. Puppies should be handled daily to ensure that they are thriving and to keep them used to human contact.

In most breeds, puppies' eyes usually open at around ten days. Basenji puppies' eyes usually open a little later; 12 to 14 days is more normal for them. By the time they have reached two weeks of age, the eyes and ears are open. When the puppies can see and hear it is not uncommon for some of them to startle the first time they see or hear a human. They should recover quickly and gentle handling and petting is good for them at this time.

In early life, puppies need the warm, dry security of their mother.

Cleanliness

Soon the puppies will begin to crawl away from the nest when they have to eliminate. It is important that they have room to do this so that they will be clean dogs for life and be easy to house-train. One good way to help with this early training is to have one part of the whelping pen warmer than the rest. Basenjis are heat-seeking missiles and will gravitate to that warm spot and consider that their bed. The rest is their "potty box" and that is the first step in house-training. Dogs that are kept in cramped quarters and learn to eliminate where they sleep are hard, if not impossible, to house-train.

Weaning

The best time to wean will depend on the condition of the bitch, size of the litter, and how much milk the dam has. Usually the puppies can start tasting food toward the end of

the third week and by the fourth week should be eating what they are not wearing. They still need their mother to feed them, clean them, and keep them warm.

Over the next few weeks the weaning process should proceed gradually as the pups depend less and less on the mother's milk. They still should have her occasional company and discipline. This is the time when the company of their littermates (and other dogs) is critical so that they are properly socialized with their own species. They should receive a lot of human contact as well. Puppies should never be taken away from their littermates before eight weeks of age; waiting until they're a little older will not hurt anything.

Here is where commercially raised dogs are deprived, as they are yanked away from their families too early in order to get them to market while they are cute and cuddly. This deprivation of proper socialization can lead to dog aggression and other social problems later in life.

First Vaccinations

Basenjis are blessed with very good natural immune systems that will serve them well as long as humans don't mess them up. It is best to not start the vaccinations too early but the puppies should have at least their first in the series before they leave the breeder's home. Boosters should not be given at closer than three-week intervals. Overuse of vaccines and too many chemicals put in, on, and used around your Basenji may weaken and even destroy his immune system. After the initial puppy vaccinations, boosters need not be given at less than three-year intervals according to a recent study conducted by the American Animal Hospital

Association in 2003 (see section on Immunization in Keeping Your Basenji Healthy).

Your breeder will inform you of vaccinations already given and instruct you on what follow-up vaccinations are needed. Try to find a veterinarian that has had experience with Basenjis or at least with sight hounds.

Registration

You should receive an Application for Registration with your puppy. This needs to be filled out by both you and the breeder. Send this application to a registering organization such as the American Kennel Club. You will be able to choose the dog's registered name on this application.

If the dog you are purchasing has already been registered you should receive the registration papers signed over to you by the previous owner. Sign them and send them in to have the dog transferred over to your name. In this case, the dog's name will already have been chosen.

There are many reasons why you should register your Basenji. For one thing, your American Kennel Club (AKC) registration is proof that you own the dog. You can be proud of owning a well-bred, AKC-registered dog. You can obtain the dog's pedigree from the AKC if your breeder did not supply one. Registering your Basenji will help breeders keep track of the dogs in the gene pool and this can be useful information to them in tracking inherited traits in the breed. Even though your puppy was acquired as a pet you may want to participate in some competitive activities with your Basenji in the future.

If your puppy is registered on Limited Registration and you later decide you would like to

Puppies learning to eat solid food.

show him in conformation, the registration can be changed to Full Registration with permission from the breeder. Consult your breeder for advice on this matter and take his or her advice.

Most pets are sold on Limited Registration to be spayed/neutered. All this means is that those dogs cannot compete in conformation showing and their offspring cannot be registered. When Limited Registered they are still eligible to compete in obedience, agility, lure coursing, and all the fun performance events sanctioned by the AKC and other organizations.

When to Register Your Puppy

Register your puppy in your name as soon as you get your registration application from the breeder. If you lose it, these papers are difficult and costly to replace. When you register your puppy no one else can use the name you have chosen. Ask the breeder if he or she would like you to use their kennel name in the puppy's

Puppies need the company of their littermates.

registered name. You do not have to call your puppy by his registered name; his *call name* can be anything you'd like. Some call names reflect the registered name but many do not. Be sure the call name is short, clear, and doesn't sound like *"No"* or any commands that you will be teaching your dog.

Fees

Registering soon will cost you less. Currently (2005), the fee is $15. If you wait the price keeps going up. Twelve months after the litter registration date it will cost $50 to register the dog. After 24 months it will cost $80—so don't delay.

Pedigree

You may also receive a pedigree from the breeder. Most responsible breeders supply this information with their puppies. The pedigree is your Basenji's family tree listing the parents, grandparents, great grandparents, and great, great grandparents. It may also contain other information such as health testing, titles, the dog's color, and other statistics.

House-Training Your Basenji Puppy

Basenjis are clean by nature so if your puppy has gotten off to a clean start at the breeder's he should be easy to house-train. Forget the old wives' tale about rubbing a dog's nose in his mistake; punishing him for something after the fact will not accomplish anything constructive. The key is *prevention*. Teach the puppy where he is *supposed* to eliminate as opposed to where he is not to go. The more diligent and consistent you are with early training, the sooner you will have successful results.

The Crate

The crate is the most useful tool for house-training. It is your puppy's home within your home and the place where he sleeps, so he will not want to soil it. It is up to you to see that he doesn't have to make that mistake by taking him to his potty place regularly. Young puppies have to eat often to grow properly so they also have to eliminate often. Feeding them their meals at approximately the same time every day will assist in getting them onto your schedule. Consistent potty place visits will make training much easier.

Crate-Training

Now is the most important part of crate-training. Hopefully your puppy has ridden home in his crate. Learning to run free is easy and comes naturally; learning to be confined is more difficult and something you must teach.

Upon arriving home, carry your puppy to the spot in your yard where you want him to relieve himself. Have the crate set up in the house where you want him to have his own bedroom. He will be happier in an out-of-the-way place but one from which he can still see his humans. After he has eliminated outside take him back inside and put him in his crate.

Ignore the fact that he wants to come out and play. Don't give into your own desire to play with him. There will be time for that later. Give him some time to settle down and be quiet in his crate. A small chew bone or toy in the crate will distract and entertain him.

One-two-three-pinned! Basenji puppies love to wrestle.

A brindle Basenji puppy checking out winter supplies.

Do *not* let him out while he is fussing; this will show him that he can control you and this will lead to "crate screaming." When the puppy has been in his crate for a while and is quiet, get him out—*outdoors*, that is. Do not let him run in the house and have an accident. Pick him up and carry him to the spot you want him to use as a potty place. Once he has voided you can bring him in the house for some playtime.

How Often?

When a young puppy plays and exercises he is speeding up his system and he is going to have to relieve himself again. Take him out at intervals during playtime. Do not make the play periods too long. Puppies, like children, get cranky when they are tired so put him in his crate to rest for a while—after he has vis-

ited the potty place again. The puppy, again, just like a child, will not admit he is tired while there is something going on that interests him. You, as the adult, need to know when it is nap-time for the puppy.

Put the puppy in his crate when you are going to be busy and can't watch him every minute. This is the time when you are teaching him what he can and can't do in the house. Unsupervised, a puppy may have an accident on the floor, chew on electrical cords (a real delicacy for Basenjis), chew on something else harmful to him, or destroy something you value.

Sleeping in the Crate

Teaching the puppy to sleep in his crate at night is the easier part of crate-training. At night it is dark and quiet so there are not so many distractions. In the daytime it is harder for the puppy to sit in his crate when there is activity in the household. But this is what he must learn from the beginning. The habits formed now will last forever. Be sure they are the right ones.

While You Are at Home

Many people make the mistake of letting their Basenji puppy out of his crate all the time when they are home. This is fine for an older dog that is completely crate-trained, but with a youngster it will lead to problems. When a puppy is out all the time that you are home, this is what he is going to expect. If this has become his habit you can't expect him to go sit quietly in his crate if you get company that is afraid of dogs. Or, if "Mrs. Priss" comes to call with little "Missy Too Clean" and "Junior Too Mean," you may want to put your Basenji in the crate for his own protection. At such times you will want him to accept his confinement quietly and not act like a hysterical wild child. Crating a young Basenji periodically while you are home is an important step in crate-training.

Other training can begin early as well, and one of these early necessities is lead-training. There are easy and pleasant ways to do this (see Leash Training, page 61).

Elementary Training Begins at Home with Crate-Training

"Why a crate? Isn't that cruel? I want my Basenji to be loose in the house."

There are many reasons why your breeder recommends using a crate. One is to protect your puppy and another is to protect your sanity. Think of the crate as your puppy's own private bedroom in your home. It is his place of refuge, his place to sleep, and his place to eat. Feeding your puppy in his crate will prevent him from becoming a picky eater later in life. It will help the puppy like his crate, ensure that another animal is not going to get his food, and, when traveling with your Basenji, ensure that he has his eating place right there with him.

Crate-Training an Older Basenji

Crate-training an older Basenji takes a different approach. If Basenjis are not started in crates from the beginning it may be virtually impossible to confine them in close quarters later in life. Even if confinement is not a problem for you at home, what will happen when you need to board the Basenji? What if your dog needs surgery and is confined for the first time in a cage at the veterinarian's? In such a situation a Basenji may go into a neurotic fit, try to escape, and inflict damage on himself.

━━━━━ **T I P** ━━━━━

Schedule of Potty Place Visits

1. First thing in the morning: Take the puppy from his crate and *carry* him to his designated potty place.

2. Immediately after every meal.

3. When he wakes up from a nap.

4. After (and during) strenuous play.

5. Before you put him in his crate.

6. At night before you go to bed.

7. During the night: In the beginning it is best to take your puppy out in the middle of the night. A very young puppy has not developed enough physically to hold himself all night long and you don't want him to learn to soil his crate. Do not play with him at this time or he will not want to go back to sleep; keep this time strictly business. As your puppy gets a little older and his good habits develop you can stop the middle-of-the-night outings. Now is the time for forming your puppy's toilet habits and consistency is most important. Develop a regular schedule—Basenjis are creatures of habit.

What if something happens to you and your Basenji has to be re-homed? His chances of this being successful are much greater if he is crate-trained.

If you are attempting to crate-train a Basenji that has been used to freedom and has never been confined to a crate, here are some suggestions. First, have an appropriate crate (see Items You Will Need, page 50, for the appropriate type and size crate).

The toilet isn't your puppy's potty place or his water bowl.

In the beginning, put the crate in a place where the Basenji can see you so that he does not feel he is alone. Leave the door open. Place a favorite toy or chew bone in the crate along with a few treats. Leave the door open so that the Basenji can investigate the crate on his own. If he doesn't want to investigate the inside of the crate, try putting his food dish in front of it for his next meal. At the following meal, put his food dish inside at the back of the crate.

Occasionally throw treats into the crate for him to go in after. When your Basenji is comfortable about going in and out of the crate, it is time to start confining him. The best time for the first confinement is when the Basenji is tired, such as after a period of play, exercise, and elimination. Sit by the crate and toss in a treat. Close the door for just a few seconds and open it again. When he comes out do *not* praise him or even talk to him. You do not want him to think coming out of the crate is something he will be rewarded for. Repeat the exercise and gradually increase the time the door is shut.

Each time your dog goes into his crate for a treat, give the command you plan to use when you want him to go into his crate. *"Crate," "Kennel up,"* or *"Go home"* are some commonly used commands.

Stay where your Basenji can see you for the early lessons in crate-training. When your Basenji is content to stay confined for longer periods of time, you can start going out of sight for short periods. He will be more content if he has a bone in his crate to chew on. When he is used to you being out of his sight, you may wish to move the crate to a more convenient location. This training needs to be done gradually and the speed with which you can progress will be determined by the stability of the Basenji.

Note: Dogs should never be crated longer than they can control their bladder and bowels.

Time-outs

Your crate-trained Basenji can be crated if he is getting excessively rowdy, nipping, or being a pain about seeking attention. *But never* use the crate as punishment. Time-outs should be given as unemotionally as possible so as not to be perceived as punishment. The crate must remain a safe, comfortable, and happy place.

Bringing Your Puppy Home

You are prepared to bring the new puppy home. You have gotten a secure crate (kennel, if you prefer) with a Basenji-proof latch, an appropriate collar and lead, food and water bowls, and toys (see Items You Will Need, page 50). You have a supply of the food your breeder recommended and have done your homework learning about the breed. So you're all set.

The more you learn about your new investment the more questions you will have. It is a good idea to have a little notebook in which to write them all down so that you will not forget to ask the breeder any last-minute questions.

This is an exciting time for everyone—including the puppy. You can't wait to get him home to play with and enjoy him—but let's not overdo it. Don't let your enthusiasm override your common sense about what is best for the puppy. Remember—everything your puppy experiences for the next few months is going to shape him for the rest of his life. Stop and think if that cute little thing he is doing now is going to be so cute when he is a full-grown dog with a mind of his own. Here is one very important tip to remember at this crucial time in your puppy's life—*use the crate!* (see Training Your Basenji, page 61, for more on crate-training).

All Basenjis should have their own private crate. This one works well in the home or vehicle.

As Your Puppy Grows

Feeding

The earliest weeks are the hardest as puppy is eating so often. As your Basenji grows, you can give him bigger meals less often. This shift in schedule will make your life easier as fewer meals mean fewer trips to the potty place. Your bigger puppy will be able to hold himself

Basenjis like cuddle beds, but puppies still need to be supervised when not in their crates.

Basenjis can be chewers, especially when they are puppies.

for longer periods of time. If you keep his feeding times consistent, your Basenji will adjust quickly to the new schedule.

By four months of age your Basenji puppy should be eating only twice a day and by six months he can go to one meal a day. Around five months of age is a good time to change from puppy to adult food, as now your puppy has cut his adult teeth and is not growing at such a rapid rate. Basenjis are physically mature by nine to ten months of age, but mentally they are still puppies with short attention spans and a propensity for getting into trouble. Be patient and persistent with your training.

Spay/Neuter

Ten months to one year is a good age to spay/neuter Basenjis as they have reached full sexual maturity. They no longer need those hormones for growth and development and altering them at this age prevents any of the problems of a sexually mature adult.

Constant socialization with humans and other dogs is more crucial to the Basenji than to most other breeds. Your puppy will grow into a well-rounded adult if you can expose him to as many different things as possible while he is young. He needs to meet different dogs and other animals as well as all kinds of people—children as well as adults. Read and use the section on Leash-Training (pages 61 and 70) so that your Basenji puppy will walk quietly by your side without pulling your arm out of its socket.

Puppy Kindergarten

If you live in an area where the local kennel club offers a Puppy Kindergarten Class, take advantage of it. The training is not very strict and it is good socialization under knowledgeable supervision. Follow this with some basic obedience training when your puppy is a little older and you will be proud of your Basenji when he is an adult.

Items You Will Need

Crate (Kennel)

The first and most important thing that you will need is an appropriate crate to keep your Basenji safely confined indoors and/or in your vehicle. When choosing a crate be sure that there is room for your Basenji to stand, turn around, and lie down comfortably. The best size for the average Basenji is a 200-size airline approved crate—27 × 20 × 19 inches (69 × 51 × 48 cm).

Basenjis love to sleep together on soft furniture and in warm places.

If your adult Basenji is confined all day while you are at work you may want to have a 300, the next size bigger; however, you do not want a big crate for a puppy that you are house-training. Too big a crate does not encourage a puppy to hold himself. The 200 size is best for traveling in your vehicle and for crate-training a puppy.

Materials: Look for a crate that is made of high-density copolymer plastic with heavy gauge electro-welded steel door and ventilation grills. The door and grill wires should form 1-inch squares (2.5 cm) so that a Basenji can't get his paws through and can't get a tooth hold on them to destroy them. Be sure the crate has a Basenji-proof latch.

You may prefer a wire crate but they are heavier to move around and some have sharp corners that can cut into things. Wire crates with a 1-inch grid are almost impossible to find and the bigger opening between the wires of most crates allows a Basenji to get his paw

through. Basenjis use their feet like cats and can hook onto things, drag them into the crate, and chew them up. Wide spaces between the bars allow a determined Basenji to grab the bars with his mouth and bend them, although a Basenji that has been properly crate-trained from the time he was small will probably not do this. Be aware that an adult Basenji that is not used to confinement can tear such a crate apart.

Don't buy a crate that has a ventilation grill made of holes or strips cut out of the plastic. A Basenji can easily destroy this type of crate and escape. Don't buy a crate with a latch or latches that can be easily manipulated with paws or teeth. A Basenji will figure out how to open it in no time.

Do *not* try to economize and buy a cheap crate; it will cost you more in the long run. Once a Basenji has learned to escape you may never be able to keep him confined. It is better if he never learns about some of his abilities.

Gates

You may need a gate or gates for inside your home to confine your Basenji to a certain area of the home. There are many types of commercial gates available and the best type for you will be governed by the size of the opening where the gate is needed. The higher the gate, the better it will be. Basenjis can climb and jump. Try to find a gate that would be hard to climb, such as one with vertical bars. You will still have to train your Basenji to respect the boundaries set by the gate.

Chew Deterrents

Products that deter pets from chewing on things you want to protect are available. Some work better than others for Basenjis so you may need to try a few before you find one that works. Spray frequently on furniture and any spot where your puppy is inclined to chew. Have some in stock before the puppy comes home. "An ounce of prevention is worth a pound of cure."

Collar and Leash

The best collar to bring the puppy home in is an adjustable nylon martingale-type collar. (See illustration in HOW-TO: Prevent Your Puppy from Pulling, page 71). These collars are the safest. When properly adjusted they have a limited tightening ability but not enough to choke. A puppy cannot back out of this type of collar. Your puppy will probably not be leash-trained when you get him and you need to be certain that you don't lose him on the way home.

Some breeders give an appropriate collar along with the puppy to ensure that you get him home safely. Have the breeder check to be sure that the collar is properly adjusted. A 6-foot (1.8-m) nylon leash that will be easy on your hands is best.

Spray both the collar and lower half of the leash with a chew deterrent and let them dry before using them. This will discourage the puppy from chewing on his leash and collar. You may want to spray the outside edges of the plastic crate as well. While the Basenji can't get his teeth on anything inside the crate, he can chew on parts of the outside.

Tags: If you fasten tags to your Basenji's martingale-type collar, attach them to the side hardware where the collar is adjusted. Do not fasten them to the "D" ring where you attach

Basenjis are almost always on the alert.

This red-and-white puppy is watching the world go by.

the leash; not only will they be in the way when you put the leash on, they will cause the smaller loop to hang down and your Basenji will be able to get it in his mouth and chew it. Adjust the collar to where it just barely slips off and on over his head. If it is too loose he will be able to get the loop in his mouth.

Do *NOT* use a retractable leash to walk a puppy. You have no real control with these leashes and you can't get a puppy quickly out of trouble without cutting your hand badly (see Training Your Basenji and HOW-TO: Prevent Your Basenji from Pulling, page 71).

Food and Water Bowls

Stainless steel dishes are a good choice for Basenjis and come in several varieties. There are the simple bowls, but Basenjis tend to chew on these if you do not take them away as soon as the Basenji is finished eating. The heavier non-tip dishes are highly recommended.

There are hanging stainless steel bowls that can be fastened inside the crate. These make good water bowls for adult Basenjis that have to be crated for a long period of time. Do *not* use hanging bowls inside the crate of a puppy or dog that is not completely crate-trained.

Basenjis will learn to get them loose from their hangers and make a mess. Once they learn they can do this, no bowl will ever be safe.

Stoneware dishes and/or terra-cotta bowls are easy to clean but be sure to get the heavyweight ones that won't tip over or slide. These are good for water outside the crate. They are also good to feed the Basenji inside his crate; it is best to feed a Basenji in his crate (see Crate Training Your Basenji, page 47).

Dog Food

Have dog food on hand when the puppy comes home. It is best to start with whatever kind of puppy food the breeder has been feeding. There is enough stress from changing homes; the puppy doesn't need the added stress of changing his diet at this time. Ask the breeder what the dog has been fed and if all the dogs are doing well on it. If they are, you may want to continue with that brand.

There are many kinds of dog food on the market. Be sure to choose one that is a complete diet appropriate for the age of your dog. Dry foods are usually the best—you can add the moisture yourself and not have to pay extra for it.

Many foods are marketed with people appeal but since you are feeding it to your dog, buy what is best for him. Many fancy foods and treats are like sugar for a child. Stick to the basics for a healthy dog and don't kill your pet with what you perceive to be kindness.

Check the ingredients of food and treats, avoid any that are chemically preserved. Ethoxyquin, for example, is used as a rubber stabilizer and pesticide and many breeders find it prudent to avoid it in their pet foods. Natural foods are best as they are preserved with vitamins rather than chemical preservatives.

Water: Your Basenji should have free access to water although you will discover that they do not drink as much as other dogs of the same size and weight.

Puppy and adult food: Your Basenji puppy should be started on a quality brand of puppy food served several times a day while he is going through his rapid growth period. As the puppy gets bigger, go to fewer but bigger meals. After you have gone through 20 lbs. of dry puppy food it is time to change to a quality adult food. Adult Basenjis do well when fed one meal a day. They are a primitive breed that evolved on a gorge and fast diet. One meal a day gives enough bulk for proper digestion; two meals affords one more chance for the

Basenjis like to chew up plastic. Be sure they don't swallow any pieces.

owner to overfeed and make his or her pet a picky eater. A healthy Basenji will act like you are starving him—don't be conned.

An average-sized (17 inches [13 cm]) adult Basenji should not weigh more than 25 pounds (11.3 kg). The best way to determine if your Basenji is in proper weight is to take a good look at him. Viewed from above, your Basenji should have an apparent waist. Viewed from the side, he should have a definite tuckup (appearance of the underline as it sweeps up from the deep chest toward the rear legs). However, your Basenji should not be so thin that you can see any of his bones. The ribs should not be apparent but they should be easily felt and not covered with a lot of fat.

Keep the treats to a minimum; these are what cause dogs to be overweight. It's much healthier to use pieces of the dry food that you feed regularly for treats and training rewards.

Toys

✔ There are many dental toys made to satisfy the dog's chewing instinct, clean his teeth, and improve the health of his mouth.

✔ The softer toys, such as flexible soft bones, are good for young puppies that are cutting teeth. However, older Basenji puppies can chew them up and swallow them, so when a puppy begins to do this, switch to the hard nylon bones.

✔ There are hard rubber dental toys that come in all shapes and sizes but be sure your Basenji is not chewing them up and eating them. The same applies to rope toys.

✔ Sterilized natural bones are one of the better dental toys for Basenjis; they can entertain

Make certain your Basenji's toys are too big to swallow.

themselves for hours chewing on them. Be sure to get the kind that won't splinter. Fancy bones with flavoring and fillings may upset your Basenji's digestive system.

✔ Latex squeak toys are fun for puppies but be sure they do not remove the squeaker and swallow it. Most dog toys these days have internal squeakers that are safer than the ones in the surface of the toys.

✔ Basenjis like the soft, fuzzy, cuddly dog toys that come in a variety of sizes and shapes. They love them but be careful, especially if they have squeakers inside, as some Basenjis may destroy them. Puppies playing with toys should be supervised until you are sure how they are going to treat their toys.

✔ The old standby tennis ball can be great fun although most Basenjis are not enthusiastic about fetching. If you are using new regulation tennis balls, be sure to wash them thoroughly several times; it is best to get the excess yellow dye out of them before giving them to your dog. There are also fuzzy toys that incorporate a tennis ball to make them easy to throw.

Treats

The first thing you want to do in deciding on treats for your Basenji is to check the ingredients. Be sure they do not contain chemical preservatives. The best treats are still the good old-fashioned biscuits.

Rawhide: Rawhide should be given with caution and under supervision. If you have more than one dog you may need to separate them and give this kind of treat to them in their crates as Basenjis will fight over rawhide. While some Basenjis will chew on them for hours, many can bolt them down in a short time, possibly causing digestive problems.

This owner has the attention of these well-trained Basenjis. It is wise to carry treats on outings.

The natural rawhide is best; fancy colors and shapes are for human appeal—your Basenji really doesn't care.

Other consumable treats: If you give your Basenji hooves, ears, dried meat treats, compressed flavored edible bones, or anything easily consumable, be careful that he is not consuming them so fast as to upset his digestive system. These are also treats that Basenjis may fight over.

If you are feeding a quality dry food, use pieces of it for training treats. Carrots and other raw vegetables are good treats. So are pieces of apple. *Do not give chocolate, grapes, or raisins as these are toxic to dogs.*

Obesity: Do not feed a lot of treats—this is the main cause of obesity in pets. A healthy Basenji does not know when to stop eating so you need to control what your dog eats—don't overdo the treats at the expense of the basic food that is better for him. Many pet owners kill their dogs with kindness.

Grooming

Grooming Tools
• Nail trimmers are first in priority. They come in two basic styles: the guillotine style and the scissors type with rounder blades.
• A two-speed cordless grinder can be a good investment.
• You will need styptic powder, gel, or pads to stop the bleeding when you accidentally cut to the quick of the nail.
• A pair of straight or curved shears will be helpful if your Basenji's tail gets bushy to the point where it bothers you.
• A rubber curry comb or a hound–glove is best to groom your Basenji.

This Basenji's nails are being cut with a guillotine nail cutter.

• There are many fine shampoos for canines on the market; be sure to use only ones that are labeled *safe for cats* because Basenjis lick their coats (see HOW-TO: Groom and Trim Nails, page 58).

A grinder is being used to shorten and shape the nails.

The secret of a good coat is good nutrition. On a proper diet your Basenji should have a nice, bright, silky, shiny coat. If your Basenji does not have a good coat, you may want to try another brand of dog food, or add oil or a coat-conditioning supplement. A bad worm infestation can cause a poor coat, as can an underactive thyroid. You may want to check for these conditions with your veterinarian.

The good news is there is very little grooming or trimming needed with a Basenji—Basenjis are basically a *wash and wear* breed.

✔ Brushing with a rubber curry comb or a hound glove will keep your Basenji's hide stimulated and his coat shining and free of loose hair.

✔ Basenjis do not require a lot of bathing unless they roll in something offensive or get muddy. For that occasional bath be sure to use a shampoo that is *safe for cats* and rinse well because Basenjis lick their coats.

✔ Pay close attention to the inside of the ears. If dirt builds up inside the ear, clean gently with a Q-Tip. If you have more than one Basenji you may find them cleaning each other's ears.

✔ Some Basenjis have a bushy tail. Tails can be trimmed with shears (blunt-ended shears are recommended). Hold the tail between your finger and thumb and push the hair up above the bone. Trim off the excess that sticks up by cutting with the lay of the hair. Do not cut against the grain of the hair or you will get "catsteps." Do not cut the hair on the tail too short; there needs to be enough hair left to protect the tailbones.

Remember to check your Basenji's teeth for tartar buildup. While dental toys and bones go a long way toward keeping tartar down, it can still occasionally build up. Dog toothbrushes and toothpaste can be purchased, as can stainless steel dental instruments for scraping off tartar (if you wish to do it yourself). If the buildup is too heavy, you may have to have your veterinarian take care of your Basenji's mouth. This will involve putting the dog under an anesthetic to have his teeth cleaned.

Nails

Basenjis hate to have their nails trimmed; mostly they hate to have their paws held tight and still for the trimming. Perhaps some primal

Holding your Basenji close while cutting her nails will help her stay calm.

TRIM NAILS

instinct makes them feel trapped. Some Basenjis have ticklish feet. To desensitize the feet, handle your puppy's feet a lot while he is young. Squeeze his toes gently and put pressure on his pads so that he is used to having his feet handled before you attempt to trim the nails. Praise him and give him treats for being well behaved.

Be sure to cut your Basenji's nails regularly. If you can hear your dog's nails clicking on the floor, or even if they touch the floor, they are too long. Dogs should walk on the pads of their feet, not on their nails. Nails that are too long can cause your Basenji to walk incorrectly and cause stress to the joints. Overly long nails can snag and tear, leading to sore toes and even infection.

Get your Basenji used to lying upside down in your lap. It is easier if you have someone else hold your Basenji while you cut his nails but if you are doing it alone, sit on the floor with him lying on his back in your lap. He will feel more secure being close to you and that will help him relax. Praise him.

Nail Cutters

A guillotine-style nail cutter is probably easiest for a novice to use although some people prefer the scissors type with rounded blades.

Nail grinders are very useful in keeping the nails short and shaped. Basenjis seem to accept the grinding better than the cutting.

Technique for Trimming Nails

When trimming the nails be careful not to cut too close to the *quick* (the part that bleeds).

Cut off the tip of the nail below the quick (the part that bleeds).

Trim the nail to just below the quick. Accidents do happen so have some kind of blood stop on hand such as a styptic powder, gel, or pads.

If you trim nails regularly, the quick will stay back close to the foot. If you neglect the nails and they grow long, the quick will grow further down the nail and you will have to trim diligently to get the quick to recede again. Nails will need attention at different rates in different dogs, depending upon the structure of the foot and the kind of surfaces the dog is on. As a rule of thumb, nails should be done about once a week.

There are some who claim a Basenji cannot be trained but this is not true. A good rapport with your Basenji and an understanding of his nature, coupled with patience and persistence, will get the job done. Training, besides giving you a Basenji that is easy to live with, is a good bonding experience. Every dog needs a certain amount of training to be a good companion and family member. Regardless of the extent of training you wish to do, it all starts with the same basic principle. The most important reason for training your Basenji is because it establishes you as the leader of the pack.

Leash-Training Your Basenji

How you handle the leash and how your Basenji responds to it are the basis for all future training. Think of it as learning the alphabet. Without knowing your letters you would not be able to read; without good leash control you will not get far in training—it is that important! (see the HOW-TO beginning on page 70 to learn how to handle the leash).

A Basenji is very strong for his size and has an amazing amount of pull power. If allowed to learn to pull, a Basenji may pull you off your feet or at least leave you with a very sore arm.

Typical head markings on a black, tan, and white (tricolor) Basenji.

Walking with your Basenji should be a pleasant experience and not a test of strength. Basenjis pull because their owners, unknowingly, teach them to pull. If someone suddenly grabbed you by your arm and pulled you, your natural instinct would be to pull back. Your Basenji will act the same way. If you pull, he pulls. Whether he pulls back being stubborn or forges ahead dragging you along, it is not a behavior you want. *Never* pull on or drag your puppy.

There are better ways to leash-train than to simply drag a dog until he submits and goes your way. If you are constantly pulling on your dog he will become desensitized to the pulling and will learn to pull back. Soon you are in a constant tug-of-war that tends to strengthen

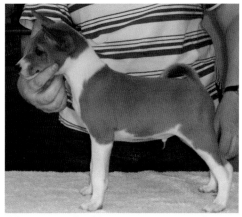

This six-week-old puppy is getting a lesson in standing on the grooming table. Even if you don't plan to show your puppy, he will need to stand quietly on a table for grooming and for the veterinarian.

your dog's neck muscles and enables him to pull harder. It takes two to pull so don't start it.

Beginning Obedience Training

The "naysayers" will tell you that Basenjis are hard to train; some even say impossible. Others will be kinder and say that they are just stubborn. When training is ineffective it is the fault of the trainer, not the dog. To be successful in training Basenjis one must understand how Basenjis think and what motivates them. Throw out your old dog training books—no Basenji has ever read them anyway.

Dog training has come a long way in the last few decades. The modern ideas of reward rather than the old-fashioned ideas of punishment are much better suited for training Basenjis. Still, conventional methods of training have to be altered somewhat for this breed. Basenjis are high in intelligence and problem-solving skills. They bore easily so the constant repetition that is used on most dogs is not good for Basenjis. The only exercise that will benefit from constant repetition is *"heeling."* But heeling can, and should, be varied with sits, turns, and changes of speed so that it is not monotonous. For all other exercises it is best to have the Basenji do it once or twice for a reward and then move on to something else. Come back to the exercise a day or two later instead of constantly drilling all at one time. This is a thinking breed you are working with, so don't insult their intelligence.

Clicker Training

Clicker training seems to work well with Basenjis although they may still have to be handled a little differently than other dogs so as not to bore them. A bored Basenji will find creative ways to relieve that boredom.

You Are the Leader

The most important aspect of successful training is your rapport with the dog. This bonding begins when you first bring the puppy home. It is critical that you establish that you are the pack leader and protector.

Some people's way of showing their dog that they love them is to give in to their every whim. This does *not* make a dog love you back; it only serves to make the dog insecure because you are putting him in a leadership roll that he is incapable of handling in an acceptable (human) way. The dog not only will not love you, he will not respect you either. Nor will he feel that you are capable of protecting him. "Tough love" is a basic animal instinct. That is why it works with children—we are all animals by nature. This does not mean that you should be cruel or abusive, only fair, logical, and consistent.

You cannot *force* a Basenji to do anything he doesn't want to do. The secret is to make him think he wants to do it. The action must make sense to the Basenji. His reasoning usually consists of, "What's in it for me?" Food is a great motivation; the way to a Basenji (and other dogs) heart and mind is through his stomach.

Puppy Kindergarten

If you have a puppy kindergarten in your area, take advantage of it. In these classes you and your dog will learn some elementary obedience exercises. Puppy kindergarten classes are geared for young puppies—mostly under six months although some puppies may be older. You will be provided with fun and easy lessons without the precision necessary at a more advanced level. The main objective here is socialization, with actual training secondary. This is the best environment you can find to socialize your Basenji with other dogs and people under the watchful eye of an experienced instructor. If a problem is developing, your instructor will probably pick up on it and can help you head it off. Don't be afraid to ask questions.

Obedience Classes

Most beginning obedience classes offer training for older puppies and adult dogs. In these classes the instructors teach you how to train your dog. There will be a specific number of classes with a graduation at the end. Usually these are weekly classes for eight to ten weeks.

Training with a class offers many advantages over training alone.

In these classes you will learn how to train your dog to *heel, sit, down,* and *come* on command.

Of course you can teach your Basenji these things at home but there are many advantages to training with a class. First of all, you will be in a structured program with specific things expected of you each week. This will help you with scheduling your training homework so that you will be prepared for class. Having an

━━━━━━━━ **TIP** ━━━━━━━━

Training Sessions

Keep your training sessions short and varied so that they are not boring to you or your Basenji. It is better to have your training sessions shorter and more often than to overdo them by working too long at one time. Basenjis work better when they are fresh. Know when to quit and keep her wanting more.

This black-and-white puppy is intently watching her handler. It is important to have your Basenji's attention when you are training her.

Food can be used not only as a reward but as a tool for instruction and communication. Use it to tell (show) your Basenji what you want her to do.

Getting Your Basenji's Attention

First things first. Before you can teach your Basenji anything you must get, and hold, her attention. This is not always the easiest thing to do with a Basenji as their minds tend to wander and the least little thing can distract them. Take a treat and work it around in your fingers to get your Basenji interested in what you are doing. When she is watching intently, move the treat up to your face and tell her, *"Watch me!"* When she makes eye contact with you, you have her attention. Give her the treat and tell her, *"Good girl!"* Repeat whenever you think her mind is wandering.

Commands

Sit

Start with your Basenji standing in front of you and kneel down to her level. Hold a treat tightly in your hand and let her smell it. Hold your hand directly above but close to her muzzle. Slowly move your hand back over the center of her head toward her eyes and ears. This will cause her to raise her head and look up.

Do not hold your hand so high that she wants to jump up. You only want to have her head move back. This will start her toward the *sit* position. Keep the treat directly over her head until she starts to sit. Say *"Sit"* as she is going down. When she is in the sitting posi-

instructor can head off any mistakes or bad habits you may fall into by working alone. The continued socialization of your Basenji and her exposure to different things is important in developing a well-rounded companion.

Whether you work with a class or at home, do not overwork your Basenji on any particular exercise. Praise her, give her a treat, and let it go till next time. If you keep her doing the same thing over and over, she will think up different ways of doing it or ways of avoiding it completely. Don't bore her and don't insult her intelligence.

When you have established yourself as pack leader, your Basenji will want to keep track of you.

Training the sit.

Training the down.

tion, give her the treat and praise her. Repeat this several times until she does it well and then move on to something else.

At a later time, repeat this process and, as she sits more readily, use your hand less and the command more until she is sitting on command. You have taught her the meaning of the word *"Sit."* The reward must follow quickly in the beginning. Later in the training she will have to work harder and wait longer for the reward.

Down

There are several ways to train the *down*; however, Basenjis do not do well with being forcibly put into the *down* position. To their way of thinking you are putting them into a submissive, and possibly, dangerous posture. It is better if the Basenji goes down on her own.

Start with a treat in your hand and the dog standing in front of you. Sit on the floor and hold the treat against the floor. Your Basenji will lower her head and sniff at the treat. She will try to get her nose under your hand, but don't give in. Slide your hand with the treat forward until it is positioned between her front legs. This will likely start her lowering her body and she will go into the bow position. Persist with the treat pressed against the floor until the rear end comes down too. As she goes down, say *"Down,"* and quickly release the treat and tell her she is a good girl. Repeat this exercise a few times and when she is going down quickly, end the session.

Training the stay.

Training the recall.

Repeat this exercise at a later time. When your Basenji is going down quickly, try the exercise with you standing up. Bend over and touch the floor with the treat hand, if necessary. Soon your Basenji should be going down when you point to the floor with your treat hand. Move from that to just giving the verbal command of *"Down."*

Stand

Use a treat to bait your dog into position. Work the treat slowly around in your fingers to keep her attention. Do not allow the Basenji to jump up for the treat. Say *"Stand"* when she is standing still, give her the treat, and praise her. If she starts to sit, back away from her and give the command *"Stand."*

To have your Basenji stand from the *sit* or *down*, hold the treat close to her nose and

then move it where the nose would be if she was standing. Give the command *"Stand"* as her body follows the bait. When she is on her feet, immediately allow her to have the treat and tell her *"Good girl!"* Repeat this exercise a few times every time you work with her.

The *stand* is a very useful command for your Basenji to know. She will need to stand for grooming and veterinary examinations. The *stand* is also one of the obedience exercises.

Stay

Start teaching the *stay* by delaying giving the treat just a little longer. Gradually increase the amount of time and give the command *"Stay."* If your Basenji breaks, put her back in the position she was in and start over. Withhold the reward until she does it right. Hold your nontreat hand open with the palm toward the dog in front of her face as you give the command to stay. This will help her understand what is expected of her.

Now that you have taught your Basenji the meaning of the word commands—*sit, down, stand*, and *stay*—you can vary her exercises and length of time she stays. Do not use the dog's name when you give these commands because the dog is expected to stay in one place. Use her name with the command *only* if you expect her to move forward such as when you are doing the *recall* or *heeling*. "*Jenny, come!*" or "*Jenny, heel!*" tells the Basenji that she is going to move.

Recall

Have your Basenji sit in front of you and give the command to *stay*. Slowly back away a few steps. Repeat the *stay* command if necessary. Call her with the command "*Jenny, come!*" When she reaches you, tell her to "*Sit*" and reward her immediately. Each time you repeat this exercise, back further away. Work toward giving all commands only once. Encourage your Basenji to come immediately and in a straight line. Have her sit quickly and squarely in front of you, especially if you intend to compete in obedience. Gradually increase the distance that you leave her.

Heeling

Now that your dog understands the aforementioned commands you can incorporate them into your walks. After your Basenji has relieved herself and you wish to do a little work, shorten your lead and bring her close to your left side. Keep her shoulder in line with your leg and don't allow her to forge ahead.

Walk forward, then stop. When you stop, have your Basenji sit squarely beside your left leg. Reward with praise and an occasional treat.

When you are ready to proceed forward, give the command "*Jenny, heel!*" In this exercise you use the dog's name with the command because she is going to move. When you resume walking, start off on your left foot because this is the leg you want your Basenji to follow. Walk and stop, giving the *sit* command. Keep repeating this exercise, as this is the one place where you do want to use constant repetition in training a Basenji. The objective is to have an automatic *sit* every time you stop. As this becomes a habit to your Basenji you can stop giving the command and your dog will sit every time you stop.

The *heeling* exercise can be varied by changing your speed. Alternate jogging with walking but keep your dog in position with her shoulder next to your leg. Don't let her forge ahead or lag behind. Vary the distance you cover between *stop/sits* and change direction frequently. Do left and right turns and about faces, where you turn 180 degrees to your right. This brings your Basenji around your body causing her to have to hurry to keep up. The about face is a good way to change your Basenji's mind if she is forging ahead or becoming distracted.

You can further vary your *heeling* by having your Basenji do a *down* or a *stand* after you stop and she sits. Occasionally release her from the *heel* position and let her wander on a loose lead and investigate her surroundings. Use a release command such as "*OK.*"

These exercises will give you a well-trained dog and also establish you as the leader. This is very important with a Basenji.

Even in repose, Basenjis are watchful of what is going on around them.

Beginning Leash Training

Do not start leash training at home. Take your puppy to a strange place, preferably a place with few distractions. A park or large field is a good place to work. Have some treats in your pocket. Be sure your Basenji's collar is properly fitted so that she can't back out of it.

Place your puppy on the ground and let her investigate. When she gets bold enough to move to the end of your 6-foot (1.8-m) leash, follow her, keeping the leash slack. At this point you are allowing her to lead you and you are walking with her and *not* pulling on the lead.

Proper Leash Control

Proper leash control on your part is important. When you

Use a treat in your hand to teach your Basenji to walk at your side without a leash.

are walking your Basenji put the looped handle of the leash over your right wrist to prevent accidentally dropping it. Gather the slack up into your right hand. Let the leash run across your body and through your left hand to the dog. Think of your left hand as a pulley. You will be using your left hand to guide the dog.

If you want your Basenji to walk further from you to investigate or eliminate, let the slack from your right hand slide through your left hand to give the dog more of the leash. If you want to have your dog closer to you, take up the slack with your right hand letting the leash slide back through your left hand until your dog is as close as you desire, then hold gently with the left hand. This will be very helpful later as you train your Basenji to walk in the *heel* position with her head beside your left leg.

Talk to the Puppy

Talk to your puppy; call her to you often and give her a treat when she comes. Then allow her to investigate some more. *Never* pull her back to you. If she is heading toward something that could be a danger to her, try calling her

back to you. If this does not work, stop the leash. Restraining is not the same thing as pulling. When you restrain the leash the puppy is pulling but you are not. This has the same effect as being tied to a post. She will quickly realize that she is causing herself discomfort and will stop pulling. If you are pulling instead of holding, then you are causing the discomfort and she will be more apt to rebel.

Keep the leash slack and continue walking with your Basenji. When she gets too far away, call her back. Use your voice, treats, or a squeaky toy to keep her attention and control her direction. Do not use the leash for control in the beginning except for restraint when necessary.

If she is not going where you want to go, pick her up and carry her—you are bigger than she is.

Controlling the Direction

In the beginning you will follow your puppy's lead. Keep calling her back to you often and reward her for coming. Gradually you will start controlling the direction of the walk. Remember not to pull. Use verbal commands and treats. Talk to your puppy so that she will be reassured by the sound of your voice. A walk with your dog should be enjoyable for both of you. After several walks your Basenji should be walking with you without pulling. Encourage her to walk at your left side.

At Home

When you are at home, in the house or your safely fenced yard, encourage your puppy to follow you without a leash. Walk with your left arm hanging at your side. Pat your leg occasionally to get your puppy's attention and to encourage her to stay close to you. Have a treat in your right hand. Reach across your body and hold the treat out in front of your puppy so that she is encouraged to follow your right hand. This will help to prepare her for more advanced training. Your Basenji puppy will get into the habit of having you on her right side. If she is conditioned to always walk at your left side, she will not be zigzagging back and forth and getting under your feet. Be careful not to step on, or trip over, the puppy until she gets used to staying on your left side.

New Places

After two or three long walks together on a slack leash with lots of praise and treats your puppy will feel confident and secure knowing that she has you connected to her and that you are never more than 6 feet (1.8 m) away. When your puppy is familiar with the place where you are training, try to find a new place to work so that you remain the center of her universe. Let her meet people and encourage them to pet her. This is a good time to introduce her to children, but be sure they are quiet, gentle children. Don't let strangers rush up to her; instead, let your puppy go up to them. Basenjis do not like pushy

Martingale collars have limited tightening, and the Basenji cannot back out of them.

people or other animals that suddenly invade their space.

Retractable Leashes

Do NOT use a retractable leash on your Basenji puppy! With a retractable leash you have no control over your dog and in an emergency you would cut your hands trying to get your dog back close enough to control her. On a retractable leash a puppy will learn to pull and form other bad habits. Also, do not use a chain to lead your dog; again, you have no control without inflicting pain on yourself. Use a soft nylon 6-foot-long (1.8-m) leash.

Collars

For your puppy, the best collar is a nylon adjustable martingale collar. When properly adjusted, they slip on over the head but have a limited tightening action that prevents a dog from backing out of them without choking her. Basenjis can wear nylon collars (martingale or close-fitting buckle type). An appropriately fitting choke chain collar is good for walking an adult dog but *NEVER* leave a choke collar of any kind on an unattended dog.

KEEPING YOUR BASENJI HEALTHY

Basenjis, by nature, are a healthy breed. While the inherited health problems of the breed are few in number, you need to be aware of them. Not every health problem is inherited so protecting your Basenji from harmful environments and giving him proper care is up to you. Motor vehicles cause the death of many Basenjis; do not let yours run loose. If they do not experience any of the inherited problems, they can be expected to live well into their teens.

Immunizing Your Basenji

Inoculations are the means of activating your puppy's inherited immune system. Done effectively, this will protect your dog for life against many canine diseases. Timing is a critical part of enhancing your Basenji's natural immune system.

Inherited Immune Systems

The first step is two healthy parents with good immune systems to pass on to their offspring. In order for the puppies to develop their inherited immune systems it is important that they get the colostrum (first clear milk

Basenjis shown sitting up very straight. Notice the resemblance to cats.

produced after whelping) from the dam. A healthy dam, immunized herself, produces colostrum that contains antibodies that will protect her puppies while their immune systems are developing. This protection can last for four months, more or less.

The most crucial time for a young puppy is between the time the mother's protection wears off and the time the first inoculation takes effect because:

✔ Inoculations given while the maternal antibodies are still in the puppy's system will have no effect.

✔ If the inoculation is given before the puppy's immune system is mature enough to handle it, the immune system may be compromised.

Basenjis often appear as if they are deep in thought.

Motor vehicles are the biggest killer of Basenjis! Don't let your Basenji run loose; keep him on a leash when outside of the house or safely fenced area.

✔ If the shot is too *hot* (contains more virus than the immune system can cope with) or is given before the immune system is mature enough to handle it, it can, on rare occasions, cause the disease to appear instead of protecting against it.

First Inoculations and Boosters

Many Basenji breeders do not give the first inoculation at as young an age as the manufacturers suggest; however, the first inoculation should be given before the puppy leaves the breeder. Follow-up boosters by the veterinarian are important and it is most critical that the last booster of the series be given after the puppy is four months of age. The only one that will protect the puppy is the one given after the maternal antibodies have worn off.

Combination inoculations should be avoided. Basenjis should receive their parvo shots separately. Canine distemper, adenovirus type 2, parainfluenza, leptospira, and canicola bacterin can be in combination as long as there is not parvo and/or corona in it. Corona is not necessary at all. *Do not give your Basenji anything that is not absolutely necessary.* Several years ago a study conducted by the American Animal Hospital Association showed that canines were being overvaccinated and given many vaccinations that were not necessary and possibly even harmful.

A minimum of three weeks should pass between shots. Until your puppy is older and has received all his puppy inoculations, it is best to avoid exposure to disease. Do not take your puppy to any place where there are sick dogs, but do not isolate him so much that his socialization suffers.

After the initial round of puppy shots, a booster should be given one year later and after that, every three years as needed. Some cities/counties require that dogs have rabies shots every year; in this case, have your veterinarian give the one-year rabies vaccine and comply with the law.

If your Basenji needs to go under anesthesia, tell your veterinarian to treat him like a sight hound (or Greyhound).

Health Problems Specific to the Basenji

Hemolytic Anemia (HA)

This was a problem specific to the Basenji; fortunately it has been almost entirely eradicated from the breed. This particular anemia is caused by a deficiency of pyruvate-kinase and is the same HA as found in some Amish families. HA is inherited as a single recessive and it takes two genes (one from each parent) for Basenjis to develop it. Life expectancy for an affected Basenji is around one to two years. Basenjis carrying only one gene can lead a normal life but, even with testing, there is no reason to use them in a breeding program and perpetuate the bad gene. Any traits a breeder wishes to preserve can be carried on through a clear sibling.

Today there is a highly accurate DNA test for Basenji hemolytic anemia available from VetGen, Genesearch, or the University of Pennsylvania. If both of your puppy's parents have tested clear, there is no reason to test the pup.

══ CHECKLIST ══

Choosing a Veterinarian
✔ Get references from friends who have dogs, your breeder, local groomers, pet stores, and/or boarding kennel operators.
✔ Visit local veterinary clinics to see the facilities and meet the doctor(s).
✔ Find out which clinics have hours that suit your schedule.
✔ Find out if they have 24-hour emergency service and where it is located.
✔ Ask about cost of office calls and basic charges such as teeth cleaning and spaying/neutering for price comparison purposes.
✔ Find a veterinarian who will listen to you about your breed's specific needs and possible inherited problems.
✔ Choose one who has other Basenji clients or, at least, has worked with other sight hounds.
✔ See if they are reachable in an emergency and are in close proximity to where you live.

Fanconi Syndrome

This is the most severe and complicated of the Basenji specific problems. The problem was originally called The Basenji Kidney Disease. Because it is like the human disease, it has become known as Fanconi Syndrome in Basenjis. Barnes and Noble's *Concise Medical Dictionary* defines a syndrome as follows: "Syndrome—a group of symptoms and/or signs which, occurring together, produce a pattern

Anything for a treat—be sure it's a healthy one.

or symptom complex, typical of a particular disease."

Fanconi Syndrome (FS) is a late-onset problem with the average age of onset being six years. FS causes nutrients to be lost in the urine and the system suffers from the loss.

Symptoms: The symptoms an owner may notice are polydipsia (excessive drinking), polyuria (excessive urination), poor condition, muscle wasting. If the lost nutrients aren't replaced, it will eventually lead to death. There is no cure. Basenjis with FS are sometimes misdiagnosed as having diabetes but if you give insulin to a Basenji that has FS instead of diabetes it can harm, and even kill, him. Be sure the diagnosis is accurate.

Treatment: There is a treatment protocol that, when followed accurately, can add years to a Fanconi Basenji's life—basically, it is treating the symptoms and replacing the lost nutrients. In order to treat a Fanconi dog you must work closely with your veterinarian and do continual testing to determine which nutrients must be replaced and in what amounts. Just as in humans, the symptoms vary from one patient to another.

The Fanconi treatment protocol can be found on the Basenji Club of America's Web site. Go to *http://www.basenji.org* and click on Basenji Health Information, click on Fanconi Syndrome, and then on Treatment Protocol. Or to receive a hard copy if you don't have Internet, write to the BCOA Secretary and request a copy of the Fanconi Treatment Protocol (for address see Information, page 92).

Glucose (sugar) is usually one of the first nutrients that can be detected in the urine of a Basenji afflicted with FS. There is a simple test that you can do at home to be alerted to this early symptom. Periodically check your Basenji's urine using urine glucose test strips such as those used by diabetics. These strips can be found at pharmacies and will tell you if there is *sugar* (glucose) present in the urine or not. If sugar is present this is not a diagnosis of Fanconi Syndrome. Sugar can be present for other reasons (bitches in estrus, for example, may show glucose in their urine).

If glucose is present in the urine, have your veterinarian run a blood test for glucose to rule diabetes in or out. If the glucose in the blood is higher than normal, suspect diabetes, although it is rare in Basenjis. If there is not an abnormal amount of blood glucose, Fanconi Syndrome is suspect and further testing as described in the Fanconi Treatment Protocol needs to be done.

FS can be inherited or acquired in humans and is probably the same in Basenjis. It is thought to be mostly inherited in Basenjis because of the high incidence in the breed (around 15 percent) as compared to other breeds (1 to 2 percent) and because FS tends to run in Basenji families.

Immunoproliferative Small Intestinal Disease (IPSID)

This is another Basenji problem that has taken on the name of a human disease. Originally it was called the Basenji Diarrhea Problem until the parallels to human IPSID became apparent. It has also been referred to as malabsorption and immunoproliferative enteropathy of Basenjis.

Symptoms: The symptoms include diarrhea, anorexia, and weight loss. Through it all the Basenjis seem to have plenty of energy. Treatment will get the diarrhea stopped and the dog eating again. Usually they will begin gaining back the lost weight, but then the diarrhea cycle starts all over again.

The symptoms of IPSID are common to many other diarrhea problems and eating disorders, so if your Basenji exhibits these symptoms don't panic. Other diseases, food allergies, pancreatitis, intestinal parasites, and various curable or treatable problems have the same symptoms; have your veterinarian rule out all other problems before you decide it is IPSID.

Cause: IPSID is thought to be inherited in Basenjis although the mode of inheritance is unclear. Environmental factors such as diet, stress, some chemical preservatives in food, lawn chemicals, household sprays, plus the chemicals we put into and on our pets may play a key role in this disease, but such factors have yet to be proven.

General Canine Health Problems

Hypothyroidism

This disease is all too common in Basenjis including autoimmune thyroiditis. The most common symptoms are weight gain, poor coats, and reduced activity level. To determine hypothyroidism the full thyroid panel must be run. This includes total thyroxine (T4), thyroid-stimulating hormone (TSH), free T4 by dialysis, and thyroglobulin autoantibody (TgAA or TAA). There are only a few labs that can run this test;

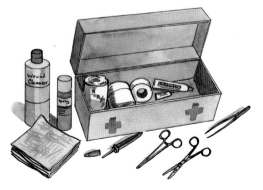

Tools to include in a first aid kit.

Board-certified veterinary ophthalmologists can check for PRA in your Basenji and the results can be registered with Canine Eye Registration Foundation (CERF).

Some dog shows offer eye clinics where you can take your dog for an eye certification.

Persistent Pupillary Membranes (PPM)

These are common in all breeds and not as serious as many other eye problems. At one time PPM was all too common in Basenjis and the Basenji Club of America requested that Basenjis with this condition not pass CERF. Over the years, Basenji breeders have made a successful effort to reduce the incidence of PPM in the breed. Because of the reduction in PPM in the breed and the fact that PRA, a much more serious problem, is on the rise, the BCOA requested that Basenjis with only minor PPM should pass CERF. Since January of 2002 Basenjis with mild PPM can pass CERF and it is acceptable to breed from them. This problem is of little concern to pet owners but should be watched in breeding.

Hip Dysplasia (HD)

This appears in only a small percentage (2.9 percent) of the Basenji population at this time. Basenjis rank 127th out of 137 breeds for HD.

HD is believed to be *polygenic*, meaning that multiple genes are involved in its expression. HD is a laxity and/or malformation in the hip joint where the socket and/or the ball are badly

there is a shorter test that your veterinarian can do in-house but it won't tell you everything that you need to know.

Pet owners should have their Basenjis tested, especially if they show symptoms. Hypothyroidism is easy and inexpensive to treat.

Progressive Retinal Atrophy (PRA)

This is an inherited eye problem of growing concern to the Basenji breed. PRA is a gradual deterioration of the retina that eventually leads to total blindness. In the Basenji, PRA is a late-onset problem with the average age of onset being six years. At this time (2005) the gene(s) that cause PRA in Basenjis has not been identified but there is ongoing research into the mode of inheritance. It is currently thought to be inherited as a recessive.

Basenjis enjoy chasing each other.

formed—this leads to lameness and arthritis. Ask your breeder about the condition of hips in his line and if the parents of your prospective purchase have an OFA number.

Many breeders test the hips of their breeding stock and register the results with the Orthopedic Foundation for Animals (OFA). You can see which of your Basenji's ancestors have been tested by going to the OFA Web site; go to *http://www.offa.org* and click on Search OFA Records. Next click on Basenji, then on Hips. Type in the dog's name and click Search. Hips that pass and are acceptable for breeding are rated Excellent, Good, or Fair.

Umbilical Hernias

Visible belly buttons are very common in Basenjis and are usually of little consequence. Usually they are small and they often close up on their own as the puppy grows. If the hernia is larger than a penny in diameter or protrudes more than ¾ of an inch (19 mm), have your

veterinarian check it. Large hernias can cause a problem if the intestinal loop gets caught in the hernia, then it needs to be immediately repaired. If the hernia is not endangering the dog most veterinarians suggest that it be repaired when the Basenji is spayed/neutered or already under anesthesia for some other procedures. Dogs who have had umbilical hernias repaired are still eligible for participation in AKC conformation events.

Inguinal Hernias

These are more serious but not as common in Basenjis; they do require surgical repair. Dogs with repaired inguinal hernias are not eligible for participation in AKC conformation events.

Parasites—Ticks, Fleas, and Worms

Basenjis do not tend to be plagued with parasites as easily as some breeds. Because chemicals and medications, put in and/or on your Basenji can cause problems, it is best not to

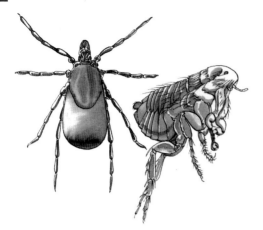

Fleas and ticks are common canine parasites.

use them unless you have a definite problem. Do not worm your dog just for the sake of worming. Take a fecal sample to your veterinarian and have it checked. If it is positive for a type of worm, worm just for that particular worm. Do not overmedicate or use any unnecessary preventatives.

Heartworm: If you live in an area where your veterinarian feels that your dog needs

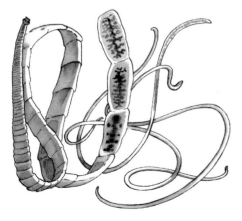

Life cycles of major ectoparasites.

a heartworm preventive, check out the side effects and the effects of prolonged use of the products available to find the safest one. Here again, the fewer things in combination, the safer for a Basenji. Avoid the heartworm preventives that also prevent other kinds of worms. The odds are that your Basenji will never have the other worms anyway. If he does, treat separately for the specific worm.

Fleas and ticks: Basenjis have very short coats and very tough skin. Usually, fleas, ticks, and mosquitoes will opt for an easier meal. It is not hard to see fleas and ticks in the Basenji's short coat. If you have a flea problem the best and safest way to get rid of them is by the use of Insect Growth Regulators (IGR). IGRs are not pesticides and do not contain chemicals that are harmful to you, your Basenji, or other animals. IGRs disrupt the metamorphisis of the life stages of the flea, preventing reproduction by preventing one stage of the life cycle from changing to another. Use of IGRs prevents reinfestations.

Insect growth regulators can be sprayed indoors and out all through your dog's environment. There are also IGRs that can be used on your dog to get rid of any immediate infestations; however, after using them in the environment the fleas will soon die off. You can learn more about insect growth regulators on the Future Pets Web site. Go to *http://www.pet-expo.com* and click on the dog symbol. Type in Insect Growth Regulators where it says "Search" and click Go.

Many Basenji breeders have had great success with IGRs. However, if you have another breed as well as Basenjis, and particularly if you have cats, the flea infestation may require stronger treatment.

Basenjis often assume the Anubis position.

SPECIAL ACTIVITIES FOR YOU AND YOUR BASENJI

There are many activities that you and your Basenji can enjoy together. While some people show in conformation, there are also many performance sports in which Basenji owners can become involved.

Obedience

Obedience training is the basis for everything you will want to do with your Basenji as a pet or as a competitor in dog sports. Most pet owners train obedience in order to have a well-behaved pet that they can control.

Although Basenjis are not known for being good obedience dogs, they can be competitive in the sport of obedience and have earned all titles available in competition.

Beginning Obedience

Beginning obedience is taught with the dog on leash. It involves *heeling*, automatic *sits*, left and right turns, about turns, and figure eights. The dog is asked to *recall* (*come* and *sit* in front of the handler) and *finish* (go to *heel*

Basenjis are entertaining. They can be trained to do many things and also can learn many tricks on their own.

position on command). He must also do timed long *sits* and *downs* without breaking.

Advanced Training

Advanced training is the repeat of the above with exercises done off leash as well as on leash. Obedience competition gets increasingly harder in the advanced classes as more difficult exercises are added. Dogs are asked to take jumps as directed, retrieve on the flat, and retrieve over jumps. Further advanced training teaches scent discrimination and the retrieving of specific articles.

Scoring

Obedience competition is very precise and regimented. The judge uses a perfect score for the exercises and deducts points for any deviation. Usually these deductions are for handler error. The dog with the highest score will get first place. There are four placements and dogs

Most Basenjis excel in lure coursing.

not in the ribbons that get qualifying scores will be credited. Titles are awarded based on the dog earning qualifying scores.

A Basenji going through a tunnel in agility.

Rally Obedience

Rally obedience has become popular. It does mostly the same exercises but is not as formal and the handler can interact more with the dog than in regular obedience.

Even if you do not intend to compete in obedience, basic obedience training will get you headed in the right direction for everything you wish to do with your Basenji.

Agility

Agility is a timed event in which the handler directs his dog over and through an obstacle course. The obstacles include jumps, weave poles, tunnels, "A" frame, catwalk, pause table, and teeter-totter.

Many Basenjis hold agility titles. The breed does well in this sport because it is a fast-

A Basenji taking a jump in agility.

paced sport that doesn't allow time for boredom. Classes are offered for dogs at all stages of training.

Tracking

Basenjis have earned Tracking Dog and Tracking Dog Excellent titles. While Basenjis have an acute sense of smell, tracking, to the letter of the law, goes against their logic. It can be difficult to train a Basenji to track.

To earn a tracking title a dog must follow a track that is laid out from start to finish with a number of turns. The dog is expected to follow the ground scent track on the path where the track was laid and go around all the turns. Scents can become airborne and shift about. With the Basenjis' keen scenting ability, they

Lure coursing provides your Basenji with a chance to show off his hunting skills.

This lure coursing Basenji is in the extension phase of the double suspension gallop and is airborne with no feet touching the ground.

are inclined to take short cuts—when they pick up the scent of the object that they are supposed to find they want to go right to it. It makes no sense to them to detour around turns B and C if they can go straight from A to D and complete their objective much easier. The smarter the animal, the harder it is to train them to go against their intelligence.

Straight Line Racing

Racing has come into vogue in recent years and is spreading to many parts of the country. Basenjis are eligible to run under the rules of the Large Gazehound Racing Association (LGRA). Hounds must run muzzled, break from a starting box, and race against others of their own breed for a given distance. Here it's all about the speed.

Basenjis are amazingly fast for their size and many have earned LGRA racing titles.

Oval Track Racing

Oval track racing is offered in different parts of the United States and other parts of the world. In this country oval racing is run under the rules of the National Oval Track Racing Association (NOTRA). Dogs must run muzzled. NOTRA records Lifetime Achievement, Top Ten by breed awards, and awards racing titles.

Lure Coursing

Lure coursing is a simulated hunt in which hounds chase a lure as opposed to live game. The American Sighthound Field Association (ASFA, founded in 1972) started this sport for the purpose of preserving and further developing the natural beauty, grace, speed, and coursing skills of the sight hounds.

Dog shows exhibit only one facet of our multidimensional hounds. Lure coursing trials demonstrate the hound's soundness and abili-

The Basenji in the yellow blanket is in the contracted phase of the double suspension gallop with no feet touching the ground.

ties of speed, agility, endurance, enthusiasm, and instinct to follow moving prey by sight. These are the attributes that are judged in trial competitions; it's more than just speed. The field trials are a good test for breeders to evaluate their breeding programs to be sure they are preserving the sight hound's natural heritage.

Note: Basenjis were not among the original sight hounds recognized by ASFA. It was not until 1979 that Basenjis were allowed to run in ASFA competition.

After ASFA had the sport well established, the AKC became involved in lure coursing. The running on the field is the same as with ASFA and the dogs are judged on the same merits. However, the classes, scoring, and titles are different so as to be more in line with the AKC dog shows.

Basenjis have earned all the titles offered by both ASFA and AKC. Lure coursing is a good

way to enjoy your Basenji in the great outdoors and meet others with similar interests.

Therapy Dogs

Basenjis make good therapy dogs. Their intuitive nature enables them to recognize when their owners are out of sorts and they are quick to give comfort. It has been clinically proven that through petting, touching, and talking to animals, patients' blood pressure is lowered, stress is relieved, and depression is eased. Basenjis, being clean and short-haired, make good therapy dogs to visit nursing homes, hospitals, and other places where people are in need of comfort.

TDI

There are Basenjis that hold therapy dog certification to allow them to enter the establishments where they are needed. In order to

Basenjis are natural therapy dogs. Those trained to pass the TDI test have access to nursing homes, hospitals, and other facilities where their comfort is needed.

think how sad it would be if you never could touch a dog again!

Temperament Test Certificates (TT)

At the end of 2004, 103 Basenjis had earned a TT number and certificate. The American Temperament Test Society, Inc. (ATTS) has developed a test that checks the aspects of stability, shyness, aggressiveness, friendliness, the dog's instinct to protect his handler, and/or self-preservation in the face of a threat. The test is designed for all breeds but takes into consideration the individual breed's inherited tendencies.

In his article, "The Psychological Basis of Temperament Testing," W. Handel, a German police dog trainer, defines temperament as: "—the sum total of all inborn and acquired physical and mental traits and talents which determines, forms and regulates behavior in the environment."

The ATTS temperament evaluation can aid pet owners by giving them insight into their dog's behavior. It can have an influence on breeding programs by educating owners about their dog's behavioral strengths and weaknesses. The ten-step test gauges the dog's responses to the following stimuli: auditory, visual, tactile (unusual footing), and protective behavior.

Note: If you plan to take your Basenji through an ATTS test it is best to find one where the evaluator has firsthand knowledge

qualify as a therapy dog, they had to pass the test given by a certifying organization, such as Therapy Dog International, Inc. (TDI). Their volunteers certify and train therapy dogs. They have visited hundreds of thousands of needy Americans, including families and relief workers after the bombings of the Murrah Federal Building in Oklahoma City in 1995, as well as in Washington, D.C. and New York City after 9/11.

TDI continues to do studies of the human-animal bond in order to bring comfort to those who need it. Nursing home residents, often deprived of acceptance and love, respond to the unconditional love given to them by a therapy dog. Without the use of drugs, these four-footed therapists give to people something medical science cannot. Touching and talking to animals gives a boost to the human spirit.

Therapy dog volunteers provide access to animals for people who would be otherwise deprived of being around them. It adds a sparkle to their day when they are reminded of pets they have had in the past and they can touch and feel something alive that is glad to see them. The volunteers in the program and the dogs that visit with those in-care facilities do make a difference in the quality of life. Just

of Basenjis because Basenjis react differently than other breeds to some of the stimuli.

Canine Good Citizen Certificates (CGC)

Basenjis can and do earn Canine Good Citizen Certificates. The CGC is a test developed in 1989 by the American Kennel Club. It is designed to reward dogs that have good manners at home and in the community. The CGC is a two-part program; the first part stresses responsible pet ownership for owners by checking to see if the dog is licensed, up-to-date on shots, clean, and well cared for; the second part looks for basic good manners in the dogs. This involves a ten-step exercise to check the dog's reaction to people, crowds, and other dogs. The dogs are expected to walk on loose leashes, to *sit, down,* and *stay* on command, and to *come* when called. They must undergo a supervised separation from the handler without showing undue stress.

This is a good project for you and your Basenji to undertake even if you do not plan any further training. Owners may train for the CGC by themselves, take CGC training classes, or beginners' obedience classes. CGC training and testing can also be used as a prerequisite to therapy dog certification.

Both purebred and mixed dogs are eligible for this program. Dogs may be any age as long as they are old enough to have received necessary immunizations such as rabies vaccines.

Basenjis as Hunting Dogs

While not many Basenjis are used for hunting in the United States today, this does not

Basenjis will stand on their hind legs or leap into the air in order to look for game in high grass.

mean they cannot do the job. With a growing population taking over much of the countryside, there are few places where it is safe to let hunting dogs run free.

In the 1960s Major (Ret.) A. L. Braun (Henty P'Kenya Kennels, Michigan) bred and hunted with Basenjis. In England, Mr. Fred Jones, the Queen's forester for many years, used Basenjis to hunt the pesky hare that threatened the seedlings.

Basenjis make good gundogs and prefer to work close to the hunter, rarely getting out of gun range. Basenjis have been trained to point, flush, chase, and retrieve. They have been used on such game as rabbit, squirrel, quail, and pheasant. Basenjis are capable of running down and catching a rabbit that is too far from its hole. One Basenji was known to have

Basenjis like to observe their world from high places.

In shows (conformation), the judge examines Basenjis on the table.

chased a fleet-footed pheasant down a corn row until it broke cover and tried to take off. The Basenji leaped into the air, pulled down the bird, pinned it to the ground, and held it until the hunter caught up.

A local Basenji club in Minnesota (no longer in existence) held scent hound trials with their annual Specialties during the 1970s. A scent hound trial was held in 1991 on the Field Day of the BCOA National Specialty as part of an All-Around Hound Award. Unfortunately, nothing else has ever been done in the way of scent trials for Basenjis.

Conformation Shows

Many pet Basenjis are not eligible to be shown because they have been sold on Limited Registration (see page 43). If you want to show your Basenji in conformation tell the breeder this up front and buy a show dog that has Full Registration.

Conformation is a beauty pageant for dogs that follows a process of elimination. The dogs are shown in classes with others of the same breed and are judged for their closeness to their breed's standard of perfection. The best of each sex from the regular classes receives points toward their Championships. These two then compete against the Champions for Best of Breed and Best of Opposite Sex. The Best of Breed winner goes on to compete in the Group.

There are seven groups at this time, with the Basenji being in the Hound Group. The first-place winners in each group then compete for Best In Show.

The handler is gaiting her Basenji so that the judge can evaluate the movement.

Organizations

American Kennel Club
260 Madison Avenue
New York, NY 10016
(212) 696-8200
http://www.akc.org

American Sighthound Field Association
http://www.asfa.org

ASPCA Animal Poison Control Center
http://www.apcc.aspca.org
(888) 426-4435

American Temperament Test Society, Inc.
P.O. Box 906
Jackson, GA 30233
(770) 354-2102
http://www.atts.org

Basenjis like a coat or sweater in cold weather.

Basenji Club of America
http://www.basenji.org
Anne Graves (Current Secretary—2005)
5102 Darnell
Houston, TX 77096
rgraves2@houston.rr.com
(713) 667-1266

Basenji Rescue and Transport, Inc. (BRAT)
http://www.basenjirescue.org
Toll-free phone number: 1-877-488-4328
BRAT-HELP@lists.basenjirescue.org

Canine Eye Registration Foundation (CERF)
http://www.vmdb.org/cerf.html

Large Gazehound Racing Association (LGRA)
http://www.lgra.org

National Oval Track Racing Association (NOTRA)
http://www.notraracing.org

Orthopedic Foundation for Animals (OFA)
http://www.offa.org

Therapy Dogs, Inc.
P.O. Box 5868
Cheyenne, WY 82003
http://www.therapydogs.com

Therapy Dogs International, Inc.
http://www.tdi-dog.org

Periodicals

The Basenji (Bimonthly)
P.O. Box 182397
Shelby Township, MI 48318
http://www.thebasenji.com
(586) 612-0279

Basenjis enjoy a good run in the park.

The Official Bulletin of the Basenji Club of America (Quarterly—comes with BCOA membership)

Books

Evergreen Basenji Club. *Basenji Owners Manual. http://www.basenji.org/ebc.*

Ford, Elspet. *The Complete Basenji.* New York: Howell Book House, 1993.

Shafer, Jack, and Bob Mankey. *Basenjis.* Neptune City, NJ: T.F.H. Publications, Inc., 1990.

Pamphlets

"A Review of the Basenji Standard," prepared by the Basenji Club of America, January 1991 Available from the BCOA Treasurer, Laura Hesse
278 W. Washington
Poynette, WI 53955
laura_hesse@charter.net
(608) 692-0414

Online Pet Products

Future Pets
http://www.pet-expo.com

Pet Edge
P.O. Box 128
Topsfield, MA 01983
http://www.PetEdge.com

About the Author

Mary Lou Kenworthy has owned, bred, and trained Basenjis. She has competed with them in shows for the past 40 years. She has also written articles on the breed and lure coursing, as well as several novels. This book is her first for Barron's.

Acknowledgments

The author would like to thank the following for their help: Sally Ann Smith, Angel Smith, and all who generously offered the use of their photographs. Thanks and appreciation go to all of the wonderful Basenjis that I have known over the years. They have taught me so much.

Cover Photos

Pets by Paulette: front cover and Kent Dannen: back cover, inside front cover, inside back cover.

Important Note

This pet owner's manual tells the reader how to buy or adopt, and care for a Basenji. The author and publisher consider it important to point out that the advice given in this book is meant primarily for normally developed dogs of excellent physical health and good character.

Anyone who adopts a fully grown dog should be aware that the animal has already formed its basic impressions of human beings. The new owner should watch the animal carefully, including its behavior toward humans, and should meet the previous owner.

Caution is further advised in the association of children with dogs, in meeting with other dogs, and in exercising the dog without proper safeguards.

Even well-behaved and carefully supervised dogs sometimes do damage to someone else's property or cause accidents. It is therefore in the owner's interest to be adequately insured against such eventualities, and we strongly urge all dog owners to purchase a liability policy that covers their dog(s).

Photo Credits

Norvia Behling: page 54; Debbie Brown-Thompson: page 30; Karen Butler: pages 2-3, 15 (bottom), 22, 31 (right), 32, 33, 51, 52, 55, 61, 65, 69, 73, 81, and 90; Joe and Marie Chamberlin: pages 24 and 83; Kent Dannen: pages 7, 9, 10, 12, 16, 20, 21, 26, 27, 36, 46, 78, 84 (top), 85 (bottom), and 92; Tara Darling: pages 25 and 93; Cheryl Ertelt: pages 4, 6, 14, 18, 19, 28, 29, 31 (left), 35, 38, 39, 40, 43, 44, 48, 49 (top and bottom), 50, 57 (top and bottom), 60, 63, 66 (left and right), 67 (left and right), 72, 74 (top), 76, 82, 84 (bottom), 85 (top), 86, 87, 88, and 91 (top and bottom); Deborah Joslin: page 37; Mary Lou Kenworthy: pages 5, 41, 42, 45, 53, and 62; Pets by Paulette: pages 17 and 74 (bottom); Stine Ringvig: pages 15 (bottom), 23, 56, 79, and 89; and Angel Smith: page 64.

All inquiries should be addressed to:
Barron's Educational Series, Inc.
250 Wireless Boulevard
Hauppauge, NY 11788
www.barronseduc.com

Library of Congress Catalog Card No. 2005053029

ISBN-13: 978-0-7641-3264-3
ISBN-10: 0-7641-3264-4

Library of Congress Cataloging-in-Publication Data
Kenworthy, Mary Lou.
    Basenjis : everything about history, purchase, care, training, and health / Mary Lou Kenworthy ; full-color photographs, illustrations by Michele Earle-Bridges.
        p. cm.
    Includes bibliographical references and index.
    ISBN-13: 978-0-7641-3264-3 (alk. paper)
    ISBN-10: 0-7641-3264-4 (alk. paper)
    1. Basenji. I. Title.

SF429.B15K46   2006
639.753'6—dc22   2005053029

Printed in China
9 8 7 6 5 4 3 2 1